Trauma in Schools and Communities

Trauma in Schools and Communities uses the power of first-hand, auto-biographical narratives to illustrate the advantages and pitfalls of specific interventions implemented in the wake of tragedies. This book addresses short- and long-term impacts of traumatic events and the challenges both survivors and responders face, using case studies from the 1995 Oklahoma City bombing; the Gulf War; the September 11, 2001 terrorist attacks; Hurricanes Katrina and Rita; student suicides; the killing of a teacher; and the shootings at Sandy Hook Elementary, Virginia Tech, and Chardon, Ohio, among others. Each story features reactions and lessons that are unique and support specific, multidisciplinary, structured interventions that should be a part of every crisis team's protocol and every community's recovery effort. An appendix features a summary of the lessons learned, a "what if?" scenario, time-specific trauma recovery interventions, a fan-out meeting agenda, a traumatic event crisis intervention plan, and answers to questions commonly asked by students about suicide.

William Steele, PsyD, MSW, is the founder of the National Institute for Trauma and Loss in Children (TLC), established in 1990 and a program of the Starr Global Learning Network since 2009. He trained the 6,000 TLC-certified trauma specialists now practicing TLC's interventions in fifty-five countries and developed, authored, field-tested, and researched trauma-specific, evidence-based school and agency intervention programs for children, adolescents, and adults.

Trauma in Schools and Communities

Recovery Lessons From Survivors and Responders

WILLIAM STEELE

Routledge
Taylor & Francis Group

NEW YORK AND LONDON

First published 2015
by Routledge
711 Third Avenue, New York, NY 10017

and by Routledge
27 Church Road, Hove, East Sussex BN3 2FA

Routledge is an imprint of the Taylor & Francis Group, an informa business

Library of Congress Cataloging-in-Publication Data
Steele, William.
    Trauma in schools and communities : recovery lessons from survivors and
responders / by William Steele.
        pages cm
    1. Disasters—Psychological aspects.   2. School violence—Psychological
aspects.   3. Psychic trauma—Treatment.   4. Disaster victims—Mental
health.   5. Students—Mental health.   6. First responders—Mental
health.   7. Crisis intervention (Mental health services)   I. Title.
    BF789.D5S667 2015
    155.9′35—dc23
    2014045893

ISBN: 978-1-138-83950-2 (hbk)
ISBN: 978-1-138-83951-9 (pbk)
ISBN: 978-1-315-71605-3 (ebk)

Typeset in Avenir and Dante
by Apex CoVantage, LLC

Printed and bound in the United States of America by Publishers Graphics,
LLC on sustainably sourced paper.

To all the professionals faced with the challenging and sometimes overwhelming reactions of school staff, students, their families and communities following tragic and traumatic incidents. The dedication, commitment and sacrifices you make to help survivors discover their strength and resilience, in the midst of great pain, echoes the spirit of your generosity and the compassion in your heart.

Contents

Foreword

It is a rare week in the United States that one does not hear about a deadly or potentially deadly attack in a school or university by a current or previous student. The traumatic impact of such incidents is long lasting. Yet, as pointed out by Dr. Steele, in his timely and poignant book on "Trauma in Schools and Communities: Recovery Lessons From Survivors and Responders," the long-term impact can be minimized if we can learn from the various tragic incidents listed in this book. What are some of these important lessons?

The first and overarching lesson is to *be prepared*. Traumatic incidents can happen anywhere and anytime. It is the responsibility of each school administrator to make sure that his/her school community—teachers, students, parents and staff—know what to do in case of potential traumatic incidents. While most incidents cannot be predicted beforehand, forming an active crisis response team and providing its members with appropriate and updated training goes a long way in coping with any potential crisis. Having each team member familiar with one's role, responsibilities, tasks and helpful recovery interventions is one of the most important lessons that need to be learned.

Part of being prepared is being able to address the developmental needs of those in crisis. Responding to first graders who witnessed the murder of teachers and fellow students, as was true for those at Sandy Hook Elementary School in Newtown, Connecticut, is very different than responding to university students and faculty impacted in a tragic shooting, as at Virginia Tech. Knowing that cognitive approaches are more developmentally appropriate for teenagers and young adults, while sensory-based, nontalking interventions are more appropriate for younger students needs to be part of the knowledge base of all those who may be involved in helping traumatized individuals.

Furthermore, knowing that regardless of one's age there are times where no amount of words is enough, but that feelings can be best expressed through art, music or other expressive activities is part of one's preparation in helping survivors of trauma.

A critical aspect of being prepared is *how to respond to today's world of immediate communication* via social media and the omnipotence of mass media. The author recommends that general statements in response to possible incidents can be prepared before crises occur; moreover, using social media to connect with staff and students during and after a traumatic incident is appropriate in this day and age. Honest, timely and accurate communication is essential in a crisis situation, yet, how many administrators are ready to do so?

Another critical issue is *how to memorialize the traumatic incident.* As the author points out, physical reminders of a traumatic event can sustain and prolong unwanted reactions and memories. Yet, no one wants to forget or ignore what has happened. There are no easy answers to some of the questions—yet, answers are needed and these difficult questions need to be raised and addressed over time. As an eyewitness to the tragedy of September 11 in New York City, I found myself being a detached observer to the various attempts to develop a memorial site and a museum that would respond to the diverse needs of the different stakeholders. Thirteen years later, there are still controversies surrounding how best to commemorate the victims—differences of opinion that may never be fully resolved.

An important reminder in this helpful book is the importance of self-care for both professionals and volunteers dealing with the aftermath of school-related trauma.

It is critical to remember that trauma responders are vulnerable to compassion fatigue and in some cases vicarious trauma in which their reactions mimic those whom they are trying to help. It is important to encourage helpers to learn to take care of themselves so that they do not become part of the problem, but are an effective part of the solution.

This book offers answers to many critical questions that are an unfortunate reality in today's world. It should be read carefully by all concerned about survivors of all ages, the impact on community and those caring for survivors in the aftermath of trauma.

Shulamith Lala Ashenberg Straussner, DSW, LCSW
New York University Silver School of Social Work

Acknowledgments

I want to thank Dr. Caelan Kuban, Director of the National Institute for Trauma and Loss in Children (TLC), a program of the Starr Global Learning Network. Without her assistance and support this resource would not have been written.

I want to thank Shanna Bellow, Nancy Buyle, Paul and Noreen Brohl, Barbara Dorrington, Barbara Desjardins, Nancy Driscoll, Florence Ernzen, Elizabeth Hasse, Randy Herman, Francine Lelande and Mary McHenry for the long hours of editing my lengthy sentences and for their many suggestions regarding the format and the lessons presented. Mary McHenry, Nancy Buyle, Paul and Noreen Brohl and Florence Ernzen— thank you so much for the twenty some years of assisting me with so many of the resources we developed together. I especially want to thank Barbara Dorrington for her always inspiring emails, numerous references and her detailed personal responses to what the stories throughout the text were teaching her.

There are so many contributors to this work: the many schools visited over the years, administrators, school counselors, social workers, psychologists and teachers who often were not prepared for all that happened, yet showed tremendous resilience and compassion in their efforts to help. There were many community responders and survivors who courageously shared their stories, what they were least prepared for, the challenges they faced when responding to situations both physically and emotionally overwhelming, the struggles they personally experienced and the effects of the demands of caring for those in crisis, sometimes at the expense of their own self-care. I am grateful to all of you for the lessons you have shared, lessons I hope this work passes forward to the next generation of crisis team members and responders who are called upon to bring the best of trauma-informed practices to those in crisis.

Contributors

I am especially appreciative of the contributions of the following profession-als who were willing to revisit their very difficult experiences and share the many lessons they learned from the day-to-day challenges they faced. You have revealed what is rarely, if ever, written about, addressed in print or in our efforts to prepare responders, yet so critical to our being prepared to protect survivors of all ages and to help them discover the resilience to move forward despite the tragedies they have experienced.

Barbara Dorrington, social worker, and **Barbara Desjardins**, principal, both of whom cared for so many left homeless after Hurricanes Katrina and Rita.

Elizabeth Haase, volunteer facilitator of the Pentagon family support groups and a licensed psychologist in Washington, DC.

Pierre Lehmuller, past executive director of New York Elementary School Principals Association, **Grace Julian**, past principal of Murry Bergtraum High School, **Sheila Brown**, past community schools guidance counselor and **Marjorie Robbins**, past director of Pupil Personnel Services—all of whom were 9/11 responders.

Dr. Anthony Salvatore, past assistant principal of Newtown Middle School and **Susan Connelly**, school counselor at Newtown Middle School, who played integral roles in the recovery efforts following the horrid loss of life at Sandy Hook Elementary School.

Laura Serazin and **Misty Ramos**, mental health practitioners from Cornerstone of Hope near Chardon, Ohio, who responded to the deadly shooting at Chardon High School.

Dr. Gerard Lawson, associate professor of counselor education at the Virginia Polytechnic Institute and State University (Virginia Tech), who also played an integral role in the recovery efforts following the mass killings at Virginia Tech.

About the Author

Dr. Steele informally began his work in trauma in the early 1980s when he published the booklet *Preventing Teen Suicide*. This led to requests for training from across the country. His experiences with nonfatal attempters and survivors of suicide was acknowledged in 1986 when the Michigan Chapter of the National Academy of Television Arts and Sciences awarded Dr. Steele's production of *Preventing Teen Suicide* a Michigan Emmy. In the mid-80s he also began working with survivors of homicide, which led to the production of *Where Have All The Children Gone*, which focused on childhood violence. In 1987 it was nominated for Outstanding Program Achievement.

Dr. Steele's work with children, teens and families exposed to tragic losses from both violent and nonviolent situations led him to founding the National Institute for Trauma and Loss in Children (TLC) in 1990, now a program of the Starr Global Learning Network. In 1997 he initiated a trauma and loss certification program. Today over 6,000 TLC Certified Trauma Specialists, whom Dr. Steele personally trained, are using TLC's published evidence-based intervention programs in 55 countries. These programs, which Dr. Steele developed, are now registered as evidence-based programs with the California Evidence Based Clearinghouse and the Substance Abuse Mental Health Services Agency (SAMHSA) Registry of Evidence Based Practices.

His more recent publications, *Trauma-Informed Practices with Children and Adolescents* and *Working with Grieving and Traumatized Children and Adolescents: Discovering What Matters Most Through Evidence-Based, Sensory Interventions*, demonstrate his ability to translate theory into practical, timely trauma-informed strategies. He has been a contributing author in such works as *Play Therapy: A Comprehensive Guide To Theory and Practice, Understanding Mass*

Violence, Creative Interventions with Traumatized Children, Critical Incidents in Counseling Children and in varied journals, including *Reclaiming Children and Youth, School Social Work Journal* and *Journal of Residential Treatment for Children and Youth*. He continues to train and consult with schools and communities across the country to bring to others the wisdom given to him by the many survivors and responders of all ages he has met over the years who have struggled and gone on to flourish following both violent and nonviolent yet traumatic experiences.

Introduction

Learning takes courage. It means looking at what hasn't helped and taking different paths to discover what does help. It's appreciating that there are many healing processes and more than one way to heal. It means being flexible and responsive, using responses that are grounded in practice outcomes and research outcomes. It's assuming the position of the non-knowing practitioner. It means being curious, a helper whose curiosity allows survivors to reveal what matters most to them in their efforts to heal. However, it is also about learning to use interventions within a framework that is trauma-informed, structured, safe and grounded in choice. It means allowing others to take us on their personal journeys, not asking "why" but "what." It's admitting our own areas of vulnerability, not as something to be feared, but as something that can help us discover ways to manage differently. The intent is that this work provides this opportunity for discovery.

William Steele

Recovery Lessons examines the lessons learned by those surviving and responding to a variety of traumatic violent and nonviolent situations involving entire schools, their students, staff, families and school communities. It also addresses incidents that took place outside the school setting yet directly impacted the behaviors and performance of children in the school setting in the days and weeks that followed.

These incidents include, but are not limited to,

- The bombing of the federal building in Oklahoma City
- Student suicides in schools across the country
- War and its impact on children from military families

- Child witnesses to violence outside of the school setting, as well as the tragic shootings of students and staff while in school
- Issues in New York and Washington DC following 9/11, as told by staff and survivors
- The school shootings at Newtown, Connecticut; Virginia Tech; and Chardon, Ohio, as told by staff and survivors
- The impact of Hurricanes Katrina and Rita as told by responders and survivors
- The worst wildfire in the history of Texas leaving 1,700 families in one community homeless and placing tremendous stress on school crisis teams in the year that followed
- Issues with memorials
- The challenges facing crisis team members in schools and communities
- The short- and long-term impacts on survivors and responders

These lessons have driven and continue to drive the updating of practices, strategies and protocols needed to effectively assist school counselors and community responders in the midst of tragic and traumatic incidents. Because the school setting remains the one setting where children are most accessible, it makes sense that we be prepared to provide students in crisis the kind of assistance school counselors, psychologists, social workers and administrators have learned minimize the long-term impact traumatic situations can have on learning and behavior. However, it is as equally important that community responders are able to provide the same assistance to the many families and direct victims impacted by community trauma.

Recovery Lessons addresses concerns of crisis team members and primary community responders asked to assist those in crisis. These lessons support trauma-informed recovery interventions that help stabilize those in crisis as quickly as possible.

These lessons are not about having all the answers, as there are a variety of beneficial ways to respond to similar situations. Rather it is about providing insight as to what frequently matters most to those in crisis and those responsible for the well-being of students, staff, families and other traumatized community members.

Recovery Lessons also offers the opportunity to compare the lessons learned by others with the current protocols you may have in place and the interventions you rely upon in a crisis. This will help to identify the strengths and weakness of those plans and interventions. To protect confidentiality, some descriptions contain information from similar incidents while still reflecting common reactions to the incidents described. Some descriptions focus on safety protocol, but most focus on recovery intervention needs of survivors and responders.

Chapter One

Descriptions of the experiences I have had over the years with survivors and responders of critical incidents are presented. Sometimes individuals were both survivors and responders. These interactions provided valuable lessons and expanded my understanding of what matters most to those in a crisis. These experiences include the Gulf War, the bombing of the federal building in Oklahoma City, Hurricanes Katrina and Rita, numerous suicides of students, deadly shootings, the killing of a teacher and a coach in separate incidents, the worst wildfire in the history of Texas, and numerous issues facing crisis teams and responders following violent as well as nonviolent incidents. After reading each description, I encourage you to take a few minutes to identify and write down your immediate reaction to each description. Also ask yourself, what lesson is this brief story presenting? Is there something that can be helpful in better preparing our community responders and school crisis teams? Is there more we need to learn to be better prepared? That lesson should involve a directive in terms of what you, your crisis team, school and community may need to be prepared to do or what you may yet need to learn, in order to better respond should similar situations occur at your facility or in your community. Space will be provided following each description to note your responses and the lesson(s) you discover.

It's important to keep a written record so you can compare your responses to the ones provided in the text. This is designed to be a resource, a working document that can be used to enhance your sense of preparedness as individuals or as a team and help identify the information, resources and training you may need to be able to respond in ways others have found beneficial. The accumulation of the notes you take throughout the text will then serve as a blueprint to allow you personally and/or your crisis team to develop and engage a plan of action to strengthen your level of preparedness and effectiveness.

Chapter Two

Chapter Two presents the experiences of school administrators, counselors, social workers, and mental health professionals from New York and

Washington, DC, following the 9/11 attacks. It describes the immediate impact on survivors as well as the infrastructure that day and the weeks that followed. These are stories you have not likely heard or read about before because the media emphasis was not on how area schools, their staffs, students and families were exposed to the crisis of that day and their struggles in the weeks and months that followed. There were major decisions to be made by all involved: decisions never previously considered by many. The challenges faced by schools in the area and their students, staff and families were immense. The stories told by a top-level administrator, a principal, a guidance counselor and an administrator of the guidance department are quite riveting and leave us with many lessons, personal and professional.

Chapters Three and Four

No one will forget the massacre of the innocent children and staff at Sandy Hook Elementary in Newtown, Connecticut. We all read the many stories that were told in the weeks that followed. However, one year later, long after the initial outpouring of support, we read of the long-term impact on the lives of everyone in that community. The stories presented in this part are the ones most have not heard. They are personal, painful, enlightening and at times almost unbelievable. Told by a school counselor and assistant principal, they address administrative issues, mental health issues as well as how these individuals have attempted to cope with all they experienced with the many families they knew whose children were killed and in harm's way.

Chapter Five

The killing of three students and critical wounding of two others at Chardon High School in Ohio a few months after the Sandy Hook Elementary School shooting did not generate the kind of coverage given to Sandy Hook, yet the pain experienced in this rural community was just as intense for its survivors. It was another community who never expected they would be faced with such a violent tragedy. It shattered their sense of safety. They did not have a school crisis team. In the aftermath, the mental health facility reported a significant increase in requests from adults in the community. They also faced many issues they were not prepared beforehand to face. The Chardon story presents many new lessons that can help us become better prepared.

Chapter Six

The massive killing at Virginia Tech presented many unique situations not faced by others. In some cases Virginia Tech responders challenged previously held beliefs regarding protocol and responded differently with excellent outcomes. With the school's military history, it had strongly entrenched values that played a significant role in recovery. They too have many lessons to share, lessons that should strengthen the level of preparedness of response teams and the approaches we all use in healing and recovering.

Chapter Seven

A number of *What If* questions crisis team members have asked over the years are presented. These *What if* questions help to identify the many possibilities that can arise following a crisis. They also address some of the challenges others were not prepared for when faced with traumatic incidents. General comments follow the different themes that these questions present. These questions can be used to identify

- what you might change or add to your current actions, interventions or plans for responding to the particular situation presented;
- the resources needed to support your responses to the possible situations that can emerge; and
- the possible roadblocks you might anticipate initiating the protocols in question.

Appendix

The appendix provides a variety of time-designed interventions to initiate over different time periods following a trauma. Additional supportive material is also provided such as helping a student reenter school after a nonfatal suicide attempt.

It is the intent of this book to begin a dialogue of sorts among community responders, members of your school crisis teams/disaster teams or those of you who are interested in developing appropriate recovery protocols. Responding appropriately and effectively to the variety of traumas that may occur takes a commitment to lifelong learning and finding research-based methods of intervention. The firsthand experiences, present practices, interventions and personal reactions described in this text leave all better prepared should similar situations arise.

Past Tragedies: Viable Lessons for Today's Survivors and Responders

1

This chapter presents a description of the experiences I have had over the years with students, school staff, community responders and survivors. These include the Oklahoma City bombing, issues with memorials, hurricanes Katrina and Rita, a teacher's murder, the killing of a beloved coach, the largest wildfire in Texas history, an unexpected delay in recovery, varied crisis team issues, teachable moments missed, nonfatal suicide attempters, survivors of suicide, parents of murdered children, the Gulf War, and the impact on children of multiple deployments of a military parent. Each description presents a lesson that has shaped the many recommendations made to crisis teams, survivors and first responders over the years. These lessons involve the roles, responsibilities, the tasks and recovery issues and interventions found most helpful to those in crisis.

We begin with several lessons learned following the bombing of the federal building in Oklahoma City. These lessons are as important as they were the outcome of that dreadful day when so many lives were lost and families devastated. The city schools were faced with trying to respond to the many unanticipated reactions of students and staff. Community responders were faced with an overwhelming number of requests for assistance from community members for trauma-related issues that the majority of responders were not trained or prepared to manage.

Oklahoma Bombing

Following the 1995 bombing at the federal building in Oklahoma City, I was asked to provide several days of training to the city school staff. Many of their students lost one or both parents in the blast or had a parent that was severely injured. In some cases limbs needed to be severed without anesthetics in order to free trapped victims. 168 people were killed including 19 infants and children. 200 children had a parent killed in the blast. This was a massive blast that damaged and destroyed over 300 buildings in a 16-block radius. It was heard and felt 50 miles away. An estimated 300,000 people knew someone directly affected by the bombing so the demand on mental health services was significant. I returned several times to train mental health professionals who continued to assist surviving family members. I also spent time with those who had a prior trauma history reactivated by the bombing.

Reaction

Lesson(s)

Lesson: The effects of a traumatic incident are rarely contained to its direct victims. A number of the estimated 300,000 people impacted in some way had individual trauma histories that were now brought back to life by the bombing. Staff at community mental health sites and child and family service agencies saw a significant increase in requests for services related to the bombing. The bombing activated many others with their own personal trauma histories. In the December 2013/January 2014 AARP magazine, Jan Goodwin interviewed several grandparents of the children who were killed at Sandy Hook Elementary School. Rarely do we hear about the impact on grandparents when their grandchildren are killed. One grandmother reported, "It's hard to cope with your own pain, when your child (my daughter) is so shattered. When my daughter visits us now, I hear only three car doors open instead of four . . . When they leave, I have a good cry" (p. 48). One death leaves many survivors often forgotten.

It is crucial that schools and community mental health agencies, behavioral health care service agencies, child and family services come

together to form a trauma-informed community task force. **The goal is to provide a coordinated trauma-informed safety net of services for all who are impacted by traumatic incidents. This includes schools because this is where children are most accessible for help.** This sounds simple enough, yet very few communities today have an active trauma-informed community task force in place.

Training

At the time of the bombing, mental health and other agency professionals had little training in trauma intervention. In 2012, three students in Chardon, Ohio, were shot and killed. The mental health agency in that community also saw a significant increase in requests for help from adults with trauma histories activated by this school shooting. Given what we know about trauma today and understanding that no one intervention fits every situation, the options for residents were limited. Chardon Schools had no crisis team or recovery protocol in place. They requested outside professional help. (Additional details related to the Chardon, Ohio, school shooting is presented in Chapter Five.)

Lesson: There remains a continual need for trauma education and training in spite of the large-scale efforts since 2005 by The National Center for Trauma Informed Care (2011) to increase awareness and to assist community schools and agencies to not only become trauma-informed but to be trained in various trauma-based practices.

Iconic Images/Memories

I will never forget the picture of fireman Chris Fields coming out from the rubble carrying the young Baylee Almon in his arms. She died shortly afterwards. At the time of this writing, she would have been 19 years old. In an article that talks about Baylee (Boyle, 2013), the following was written,

> The world can seem so random. It could have been a different child, or a different firefighter, or a different photographer. But on that day, in the face of that tragedy, for that time, everything came together for that one photo to define the Oklahoma City Bombing. Her mother said, "I feel like Baylee was put on this earth to do what she did, and that was to represent everyone who died in the building that day."

Reaction

Lesson

Lesson: The facts of what take place in the midst of and following traumatic situations are rarely remembered as easily and as intensely as the memories, sensation and emotions triggered by one iconic image. Neuroscience confirms that the sensations, feelings and memories of trauma are encoded iconically in symbolic forms. These iconic images reflect the fear, terror, worry, the absence of a sense of safety and feeling powerless. They shape our thoughts about self, others and the world in ways that often are void of trust, strength and resilience. They also drive primary survival behaviors that often become problematic for survivors and those around them. Before these iconic memories can be altered, they must first be externalized into a concrete form, such as in a drawing. This evidence-based practice has demonstrated repeatedly that once our iconic memories and sensations are externalized into a concrete form, survivors are better able to understand, manage and regulate the many reactions to that trauma and those elements and situations in the present that are a reminder of that past tragic incident. This focus should be an integral part of our efforts to help those who have not benefited from crisis intervention or psychological first aid (Steele & Kuban, 2013).

Physical Reminders

I also remember the 10-foot-high chain-link fence that was constructed around the bombed-out area. It was immediately filled with mementos from people who came from around the world. The compassionate outpouring that people demonstrated was amazing. There were notes, photos, flowers, key chains, even license plates and so much more. The fence remained up for four years until the memorial was completed. A number of the mementos were later included in the memorial. The people of Oklahoma showed great resilience in the days, weeks, months and years that followed. However, as many reported, the fenced in area was a painful reminder for many who lived and worked in that area.

Lesson: Physical reminders of a traumatic event can sustain and prolong unwanted reactions and memories. Those who worked and lived in close proximity to the bombed-out area or who needed to pass by that area regularly to get to their workplaces or home were constantly reminded of the tragic loss of life, the pain and shattered sense of safety. Although the chain-link fence that surrounded the bombed-out area was filled with the mementos of supporters from around the world, the reality for many was that this visual show of worldwide support still activated their fears and pain.

Memorials

There is a significant challenge when a school is the site of the trauma. Unwanted memories and reactions can be prolonged and sustained. When schools are the site of the tragedy, the question of creating a permanent memorial at the school can be a difficult one. There are some solutions to consider. Sandy Hook students will have a new school thanks to a $50 million grant from the state of Connecticut. The old school will be torn down. Not all school communities have access to such resources. After the shootings in Littleton, Colorado, Columbine High School completely demolished its library, where the majority of the deaths occurred. The site, located above the cafeteria, was then turned into a memorial ceiling and Atrium. A new larger library was built on the hill where the shooting began. The permanent memorial is located in Clement Park, adjacent to the high school. The question raised was whether a permanent school memorial would help survivors or continue as a reminder of the trauma that took place?

There is a general consensus that memorials provide an avenue for healing, a place to visit (National Association of School Psychologists, 2002). However, many people in Oklahoma told me that it wasn't until the fence was taken down and the memorial was completed that they could begin to feel as if their lives could now move forward. It replaced the trauma-related visuals with a visual that now reflected strength, resilience and hope for them and for those who would visit. It is a place of peace and reverence for those lives that were tragically and traumatically ended.

I made a final trip to the city years later after the memorial was completed. The memorial—with its reflective pool and memorial chairs (one for each person killed), and the lone elm tree that survived the blast and the fires that followed—created immediate emotional and physiological sensations. Words really cannot describe the overwhelming, yet amazingly profound sense of connection I felt with those who died suddenly that day. It brought me into the lives of all of those affected by this tragic event. I can only imagine the many reactions of loved ones.

Reaction

Lesson

Lesson: Memorials do allow people to come together to support one another, as well as express their feelings in a supportive environment. Still, research shows that for some those same memorials remain a painful memory. The question remains, "Do permanent memorials belong in our schools?"

There are specific reasons for schools not to erect permanent memorials in the school setting (Pain, 2007). From a trauma-informed perspective and for many practical reasons, permanent memorials are not recommended within the school setting. Trauma is a state of terror in which victims feel unsafe and powerless to do anything about their situation (Steele & Raider, 2001). Trauma is also often accompanied by worrying, often about "it" happening again and "will I be next?" Arousal is a psychophysiological and neurological state of readiness for the "next time." Physical proximity to the actual location of the tragedy and/or to visual reminders activate the arousal response (van der Kolk, McFarlane & Weisaeth, 1996; Rothschild, 2000). Memorials, although beneficial for many, are also activating for many, especially those with their own personal trauma experiences. This constitutes a significant number of students in any facility.

Practical Challenges

Permanent memorials can also present a number of practical issues that further support that schools are not the best place for them. Where will the resources come from to maintain the memorial, especially the larger memorials, like gardens? How large will the memorials be allowed to grow? In reality, many deaths can occur within a few years. The number can grow quite rapidly. From 1996 through 2003, Slippery Rock High School in the Pittsburgh, Pennsylvania, area experienced 23 tragic student deaths (Clark & Woodall, 2004). Do we really want students to be reminded daily of how many have died? What if the memorial or parts of that memorial are destroyed or fall into disrepair? For some students memorials help, for others they invoke negative emotions and unwanted memories.

Once the practice of creating a permanent memorial begins, how will the school respond to the politically and economically influential parents in the community who insist that their child be given a separate memorial? Are schools prepared to respond to the friends and families of students with much less status or those who have been disruptive students? Sometimes people will question the value of including a "less desirable" student to the memorial. Who is going to make the value judgment as to who is included and who is excluded? Should exceptions be made for different students or different situations? School board members change and make exceptions to past rules. However, history shows when exceptions are made regarding memorials, conflicts immediately emerge that could have been avoided.

Reaction

Lesson

Lesson: Given what we know about trauma today and the experiences of others in the past, schools might wish to consider supporting the creation of a memorial in the community. Those who find comfort in visiting can do so, while those who are uncomfortable also have the opportunity to avoid the memory. (Virginia Tech presents a different outcome that will be discussed in Chapter Six). At all times, it is best to make decisions about responses that have long-term implications before there is a need to do so. Such a critical decision should not be made following a tragedy as emotions can be intense and lead to less than objective, well-thought-out solutions. Participants need time to adequately discuss long-term implications and options.

The City Schools

Their close proximity to the blast, the massive rescue response, media and the number of students and staff who had families working at the federal building triggered immediate and varied reactions in students and staff. The city schools were not prepared for the sheer number of students and staff whose reactions needed a response. These were reactions that were not anticipated children or staff would ever experience.

Even today when conducting training, I ask participants to identify all the possible reactions their students might experience after specific incidents such as suicide, murder, a fatal car crash, the sudden death of a teacher or the murder of a teacher while in school. The responses are brief and frequently do not delineate among the many reactions specific incidents can induce, such as the differences in reactions between murder and suicide. When asked all the possible ways they might respond to each of these reactions, their responses are also limited.

Lesson: Prior to attending to the varied needs of students and their many possible reactions, crisis team members need to quickly review all the possible reactions and interventions that may be necessary. In doing so, they will be better prepared and less vulnerable to being overwhelmed by student and staff needs. This information should be part of any recovery protocol manual.

Rescue Dogs

Following the bombing an interesting story developed about the rescue dogs. It illustrates what can happen to our nervous systems when what we are trained to do is not producing desired outcomes. At one point, the rescue dogs sent to locate those still living quit working because they were unable to find survivors. In order to reenergize the dogs, rescue workers were concealed in the rubble so the dogs could experience the rescue of living survivors. Once they were able to successfully do what they were trained to do they were able to continue the rescue efforts.

Reaction

Lesson

Lesson: When interventions in a crisis situation are not producing the desired outcomes, we as helpers are vulnerable to compassion fatigue. It is critical that possible alternative interventions be easily available when initial responses fail. Equally important are self-care interventions to help prevent compassion fatigue. I met with one of the city school counselors several times in the year that followed the bombing. She was fatigued and struggling. As she and so many since have said, "I was not trained for this." **Training about compassion fatigue and vicarious trauma is an essential part of self-care.** It is certainly essential to the level of quality care we provide survivors.

Hurricanes Katrina and Rita

Hurricane Katrina hit New Orleans on August 29, 2005. By September 5, 25,000 evacuees occupied the Houston Astrodome. One volunteer described it as a "sea of cots." Hundreds of professionals, many of them school counselors, psychologists, teachers and local mental health practitioners, immediately began volunteering their services. Under federal law, Houston-area schools were required to enroll 5,000 of the children living at the Dome. This placed additional stress on the school system, its staff and students. Although the dome provided shelter and food for thousands, safety was always an issue. Old New Orleans neighborhood rivalries, now contained in such close proximity under stressful conditions, led to a number of fights causing families to be concerned about their safety. As was the case in other shelter situations across the country, behaviors related to intoxication, drug use and psychiatric issues further intensified fears and anxiety. This had a significant impact on the children. In addition, there was no real privacy. The children brought the negative impact of the conditions they faced in this setting with them into the school setting.

Just weeks after Hurricane Katrina, Hurricane Rita hit the Gulf Coast on September 24, 2005. A massive evacuation took place that created even more stress on the overburdened nervous systems of Katrina volunteers who became potential victims themselves. In mid-October, a few weeks following Hurricane Rita, I met with approximately 200 of these volunteers. Following are some of their responses to specific questions asked about the dominant thoughts that now occupied their days, their worries, what surprised them and what the worst part of the past two months had been for them. They were also asked what their thoughts were about their futures. The responses are followed by the opportunity to note your responses and the lesson(s) each presents.

I worry about:

- The teachers who are having to keep up test scores but now have kids for whom we have no records and who are not at the same academic level of performance of our students.
- Teachers who are already overtaxed with test performance and are now overtaxed by having to deal with the new kids and the problems they bring.
- Teachers overloaded with having to create EI folders because we have no records whatsoever on these kids.
- The kids who have not yet been reunited with their families.
- The lack of resources for our schools in the months to come.
- The real cultural conflict between Texas and New Orleans in ways we didn't realize existed till now.
- The fights that are breaking out and kids ending up dead.
- How I will take care of those already on my caseload. We've made advances and now I'm worried the gains will disappear because I won't have as much time with them.

- About the families overwhelmed by the unanticipated mental health needs of families they took into their homes.
- About us as volunteers, who were not prepared for what we experienced. We need some help too.

Reaction

Lesson

Lesson: It makes sense in today's world that schools have emergency contingency plans prepared ahead of time. All communities are more at risk for experiencing the large impact of trauma-inducing catastrophic events.

Imagine a school district having to suddenly accommodate 5,000 unplanned new students and the physical as well as emotional stress this creates for everyone involved. This is exactly what Houston city schools were mandated to facilitate. This placed enormous stress on the school system creating overcrowded classrooms, sharing of limited resource materials, safety concerns and lack of background information on new students. This made it more difficult to meet their needs. Cultural differences also arose that surprised many. This led to conflicts and misunderstandings. The disruption to the regularly attending students of that district, scheduling and the financial burden were only a few of the administrative, management and educational crises this one traumatic incident created for Houston schools, students, their families and staff.

On a smaller scale, following 9/11 hundreds of students were placed at other schools, creating similar difficulties for the schools taking in new students forced out of their own facilities. Even after the experience in Houston, there are school districts today that have not considered the possibility of this need. New York Schools were not prepared for what to do with incoming students from Lower Manhattan. For example, they had not considered the increased use of the toilets and the plumbing issues this caused. For some this may seem like a minor issue, yet for students and staff whose lives had been turned upside down and inside out, this was one more crisis added to an already overstressed group of people. Following are the comments of responders and what they were not prepared to experience.

I was not prepared for:

- The absence of gratitude.
- The number of kids who were unable to read or were way below appropriate reading level.
- Seniors provided a dinner for a number of families. I was not prepared for the way they left the place. They didn't use the trashcans; there was no thought of picking up after themselves.
- The folks who squandered their $2,000 Federal Emergency Management Agency (FEMA)/Red Cross allotments on nonessentials.
- The anger by impoverished Texas families over New Orleans families now getting preferential treatment, all the food, etc., and how many parents are fueling this kind of anger in their children.

Reaction

Lesson

Lesson: It is very important to identify the expectations that primary responders/crisis team members have about what they hope to accomplish and how they anticipate others will respond to their efforts to help. When expectations are not in line with reality due to the varied ways people react, responders become more vulnerable to compassion fatigue and in some cases vicarious trauma.

The hundreds who volunteered their time to assist the thousands housed at the Astrodome in Houston experienced compassion fatigue and in some cases vicarious trauma as a result of their experiences. The day I spent with these volunteers revealed they had inadequate preparation as first responders. Many of these volunteers were professionals whose education and training as professionals still offered very little protection against compassion fatigue and vicarious trauma. The realities they faced shattered their expectations and seriously challenged their own resilience. These very same volunteers were soon faced with Hurricane Rita and in the process became victims as well.

Personal Reactions—I was surprised by:

- All the crying I've been doing the last several days. It's not related to anything in particular.
- How different I acted, like I became a different person, I got so overprepared. I'm single and I wouldn't normally do what I did. I was so prepared I was waiting for it. I didn't evacuate.
- How detached I became. It was kind of surreal. It wasn't me.
- How much I'm forgetting lately.
- The sadness I felt at the realization there may not be anyone to help me in a disaster. I no longer feel safe or protected.

Reaction

Lesson

Lesson: Professionals are just as vulnerable to the effects of traumatic exposure as are nonprofessionals. Self-care is a critical issue often overlooked among professionals. As indicated earlier, interventions related to self-care need to be an integral part of the recovery process.

When meeting with crisis team members across the country who have been first responders responsible for attending directly to the survivors of trauma, I ask how many of them have participated in a formal support group process in the weeks that followed that crisis. At best, only about 5% of participants are offered the time to formally process all they were exposed to as primary responders. There still remains the belief that as a professional "I should be able to manage whatever comes my way, on my own." I have always believed that self-care and restorative support ought to be part of any crisis team protocol.

Comments About Hurricane Rita Evacuation

I was surprised by how:

- I was struggling to breathe; the heat was horrible. You didn't run your car's air conditioning because you were afraid to run out of gas.
- I wasn't prepared for people leaving dead pets on the side of the road during evacuation.
- I wasn't prepared to be going to the bathroom on the side of the road because of being stranded for hours on the expressway.
- I worried about being separated from my family.
- I wasn't prepared to totally lose it when a couple of cars cut in between my car and my son's car. I was angry because now they were threatening my family.
- I took a gun with me. I don't even know how to use it, but I was afraid.
- I worry about the next hurricane and not being able to take any more.

Reaction

Lesson

Lesson: The Houston story also points out that one crisis can be followed by another crisis. Contingency plans need to be in place. Additional help from crisis teams outside the school district are crucial in the event of multiple crises, especially one too large for the district to manage alone. Outside help is often needed when single incidents bring about repeated media coverage or when environmental infrastructures have been damaged or destroyed and are not immediately restored or replaced. **Exposure and its stressful effects will remain as long as what people have been accustomed to in their communities is no longer functioning or available as a result of a traumatic event.**

Comments About the Future:

- Given the overcrowding we are experiencing in our schools and the community, the demands still being placed on us, the fact that FEMA is so slow so there is no certainty as to when evacuees might be relocated to their community or elsewhere, it is hard to think about the future right now.
- If I think about the future right now, all I think about is what else can happen.
- I have to focus on today, one day at a time and enjoy what I can right now or I won't make it.
- The fact is we have all been reaching out to one another for support realizing we are all in this together. We will get stronger.
- Whatever the future might present, hopefully we have learned from all this that the days of going it alone are over.
- It has been really hard, but I find myself doing things I never thought I would do. I am surviving and seeing strength that I didn't know was there in myself and others.

Reaction

Lesson

Lesson: The above responses of survivors reflect fear, but also the resilience they discovered during a very difficult period. **One of the important questions to ask when briefing primary responders after their work is completed is, "In the midst of a crisis there is always something or someone that brings a smile to our face or helps us reconnect to our strength and resources. Who or what might that be for you?" When responders are unable to provide personal examples, it may be an indication of compassion fatigue.** Recently, a friend and colleague, Dr. Lennis Echterling, presented me with a wonderful example of the inner resources of survivors of trauma. He tells the story of one of the surviving victims of a land mine explosion in Beirut. The survivor introduced himself to Dr. Echterling and said, "I am not a victim of a land mine. The land mine is a victim of me. I survived—the land mine didn't."

In the Shelters

(An excerpt sent to me from Barbara Dorrington and Barbara Desjardin's unpublished journal of their experiences with hurricane survivors.)

"After spending the first few days in the shelters at Levi Strauss (about 400 evacuees) and Lackland (about 150–200), it became apparent that although there was a large contingent of volunteers in the shelter, no one in particular was focusing on trauma recovery. The children had little to do during the day, as they were not in school. These children were scared and anxious. All that happened to them and was happening or not happening around them overloaded their nervous systems; doing nothing only intensified their reactions."

Reaction

Lesson

Lesson: This is yet another example of the need for ongoing trauma training especially related to the developmental needs of those in crisis.

Children's Response:

"My colleague, Barb Desjardins, and I set up two art tables in a common room so that parents could feel safe allowing us to invite their children to a table to color and chat. During the first day or two, children were happy to come up individually or in small groups—some of them from the same families—cousins, brothers and sisters. Quickly, adults joined the table after about a day. Some adults were related to the children and some were entirely alone but wanted the companionship of a comfortable and inviting place to sit."

Reaction

Lesson

Lesson: In the midst of crisis people will do best when they are actively engaged in doing something. Neuroscience has demonstrated that trauma is as much a nervous system response as a psychological one (Levine & Kline, 2008). When in crisis, it needs to do something in order to try and regulate all its reactions. This is the case for adults as well as children. The need to do something is a way to recapture some sense of control over what has happened or is happening to us. For children, doing something that involves some form of play can help to reduce significant stress. Adults also begin to regulate their reactions when they are actively involved in doing something, even just joining a table to be with someone. For example, in school settings there are numerous activities that can be initiated. These include collecting money, giving blood, writing out cards and letters, using social media to send verbal and visual support, and engaging students in a structured discussion of what happened that addresses social implications, mental health, life in general and ways to cope. The list is endless. **It is in the doing that people in crisis begin to heal.**

Indirect Benefit of Trauma Training

Following Katrina I provided trauma training to school staff in Baton Rouge Louisiana. Several weeks later I received the following note, "I was there to learn how to help my students and left finding help for myself."

Reaction

Lesson

Lesson: This response speaks to the way trauma can activate those responsible for helping students. Professionals frequently do not realize or are reluctant to acknowledge, or get help for their personal reactions. This only prolongs those reactions, leaving them far more vulnerable to compassion fatigue and vicarious trauma. (This one experience also demonstrates that training can be designed to indirectly help primary responders, who may not otherwise realize how they were impacted by exposure to those who needed their help.)

In my trainings I now encourage professionals to participate in the intervention processes being recommended for traumatized children. This practice allows them to experience the many possible reactions children may have and indirectly gives them the opportunity to safely receive some relief from prior reactions to personal experiences or from their exposure to helping students in crisis.

A Teacher's Murder

Over the years I have worked with hundreds of schools assisting them in the development of crisis teams and crisis/trauma recovery interventions and protocol. Many developed excellent recovery intervention strategies and protocol. As school shootings and other deadly violence became a larger problem, states were mandating schools to also develop specific safety protocols. Schools have such protocols in place today. However, with such a focus on safety, recovery interventions and crisis teams were given far less attention. In essence recovery interventions and protocols went by the wayside. Previously trained intervention teams disappeared. Fortunately the importance of recovery interventions is once again emerging. They are now being seen as critical to minimizing the intensity of reactions and behaviors, which left unattended can and do lead to impaired learning and disruptive behavioral challenges from students and staff.

I met with a group of staff about one month following the killing of a teacher by a student. At the time, the building was secured immediately as safety protocol was followed. Unfortunately, this was a district that previously had a well-trained crisis team with excellent recovery interventions and protocol strategies. Like in so many other districts, these had been ignored and not initiated following this murder. I asked all staff I met with who the crisis team members were for their building. They simply did not know. The school was not prepared when the murder took place to follow what today are standard recovery processes directed at students and staff. The outcome was disastrous.

The absence of systematic, time-designed recovery responses left the staff distrustful of administration. School administrators were viewed as unprepared and insensitive to the many reactions this murder induced in staff and students alike. Despite the safety protocol that had been initiated at the time, staff still did not feel safe one month later. Their feelings of abandonment and being ignored intensified and prolonged reactions induced by this murder. All of this would have been prevented with a systematic recovery response by a prepared crisis team. The following responses, which have been discreetly altered to protect confidentiality, include those I've encountered over the years from others facing similar situations.

Communication Issues the First Day:

- We weren't even told that this was one of our teachers.
- Communication was not there in the beginning and still isn't.
- The media knew immediately.

- The students and even we were texting back and forth to find out what happened.
- There is no excuse for saying, "We're still planning." When they want something, they want it immediately.
- My mother knew more than I knew.
- The brother of the student who killed the teacher showed up for school and students and staff were not prepared to receive him.

Reaction

Lesson

Lesson: These statements reflect an absence of protocol related to when and who needs critical information about what has happened or is happening and how and when that information is to be instantly communicated to staff, students and families. **In today's world of immediate connections via social media, it is critical in a crisis that school administrators immediately connect with their staff and students via the same social media they use. Failure to initiate immediate communication will leave staff questioning administration's level of preparedness and competency to manage what has happened. Although it may not be true, it can also leave staff members feeling unimportant and that their concerns and feelings do not matter.** This was expressed in several statements. **Immediate communication with staff is expected in today's social media world. When this does not happen, adverse perceptions and feelings prolong unwanted and undesirable reactions.**

For the most part, statements in response to possible incidents can be prepared before crises take place. This information can be stored on a computer and quickly distributed via several mediums. General statements can be posted to simply let all staff know that the administration is aware of what has happened and has mobilized resources to ensure their safety as well as to help those in need. For example one statement might read, *"We are aware of what has happened and are currently mobilizing help. Please follow our lockdown procedures until we inform you the building is secure."* This brief immediate message can be reassuring and prevent the kinds of responses cited in this example. As soon as the building is secure another brief message can be sent. It might contain the following information, *"The building is secure. More help is coming. The following crisis team members are available for immediate help by (calling the office). Check for updates throughout the day . . ."*

The Next Morning:

- We needed to process our reactions and concerns at the faculty meeting the next morning but they simply told us what not to do.
- No one gave us time to express our reactions.
- They said they would let us know what would be happening and we still don't know all that is happening.
- I was left feeling no one really cared about us being scared, sad and worried.
- Administration was upset the media got information before they released a statement. We were told not to talk to the media. We got a lecture.
- There were so many different stories. As professionals we should have been given a statement that we knew we could say to media and even to our friends and families rather than be lectured.

Reaction

Lesson

Lesson: Understanding the needs of staff is essential to empowering them to engage in practices throughout the day that are supportive of students and the overall efforts to restore calm throughout the facility. There are critical issues that need to be immediately addressed and communicated to all staff at one time in a way that is supportive, sensitive to their needs personally and professionally. It should afford them the opportunity to express their concerns, clarify their roles and responsibilities.

The previous statements reveal a lack of helpful direction in response to students throughout the days following the crisis. Little thought was given to student behaviors, which might necessitate a referral to the crisis team. How to quickly access the crisis team for help, what schedule changes might be needed and a number of other necessary issues were not addressed. These statements further reflect that people were not given an opportunity to have their concerns and needs addressed. This is extremely counterproductive in a crisis.

In regards to the media and the need to have a prepared statement for staff, there are strong reasons for not talking to the media that should be presented to staff. For example, *"If media approaches you please keep in mind that statements you might make can be edited. Also keep in mind that this is a very emotional time for all of us; what you intend to say, may not be what is actually heard. The media can present what you say in ways that make you seem insensitive, unsupportive or in conflict with your peers. This will not be helpful to you or others so please be careful."* And as suggested by one of the statements, it always helpful to provide staff with a written response they can use. A prepared statement in this regard obviously needs to be brief and focused on the safety of all, outlining help everyone is receiving in words that convey the resilience and strength of both students and staff.

Safety Concerns:

- We need to know if we have students like this.
- We can't prevent what we don't know.
- I asked to look up one child's folder I was concerned about and was told I couldn't.
- I'm very angry that we don't have access to information on potentially dangerous students. This falls under at FERPA not HIPAA.
- I don't feel a sense of security walking down the halls. This is lingering, even in the presence of additional officers, because folks are not informed of students with violent histories.
- Last year we had notes on the students that gave us information regarding what works and what doesn't.

```
┌─────────────────────────────────────────────────────────┐
│  Reaction                                                 │
│                                                           │
│                                                           │
└─────────────────────────────────────────────────────────┘


┌─────────────────────────────────────────────────────────┐
│  Lesson                                                   │
│                                                           │
│                                                           │
│                                                           │
└─────────────────────────────────────────────────────────┘
```

Lesson: Instilling a sense of safety in students and staff goes beyond the physical presence of resource officers. It begins with staff being informed of the possible risks students present. Responders then need specific guidelines as to how best to respond to those students when behaviors escalate or present a possible threat. Basic human nature demonstrates repeatedly that when we leave at-risk children unattended, they engage in more at-risk behaviors. In settings that care for at-risk children and adolescents, a behavioral management plan can be developed that provides staff with specific ways to respond and not respond when behaviors begin to escalate. This not only benefits the child by minimizing the need for physical intervention, but also benefits staff. Without such information, they have no guidance on when or how to take action to de-escalate unwanted behavior.

A sense of safety is supported and instilled when adults caring for at-risk students (any at-risk individual) have some information as to what may work and what will likely make matters worse. This is especially important during a school crisis, as at-risk students may need additional attention.

Personal Reactions:

- It could be me anytime.
- I just have a loss of trust.
- When driving to the parking lot, I get a panic attack.
- I'm forgetting a lot; that's not like me.
- I just feel tremendous guilt that I can't be there for everyone.
- I've been unable to sleep—just too many memories.

- I feel like shit.
- It bothers me that his name is still on the roles.
- What do I tell my kids when we're in lockdown? I didn't know what to say.

Reaction

Lesson(s)

Lesson: These personal reactions of staff again reveal that when in a crisis they are as vulnerable as their students. Support is essential. The reactions of staff must be acknowledged and normalized. Directives as to ways they can care for themselves are also needed to help them regulate their reactions. They must feel empowered by being given the opportunity to verbalize their concerns, ask questions and make suggestions. I have conducted many such staff meetings (see Appendix for End of Day Staff Meeting) following suicide, murder, sudden accidental deaths of students in school and outside of school hours, and environmental tragedies. This process has always helped give staff a sense of empowerment. They make excellent recommendations and their observations of what went well, what was not needed or what could have been handled differently provide valuable information for the actions to be taken the following day. It allows them to feel united as a staff by discovering they are experiencing many of the same reactions. Equally important, it is this process that allows the administration to demonstrate support and concern for the staff's well-being.

Lesson: The one question about what to say to kids during a lockdown stresses the importance of training in this area. What teachers can say will depend upon the varied possibilities regarding the immediate safety and security of the students in the location they are in at that time. Basically if safe, students simply need to hear, *"We are safe now so we are going to stay here until I* *hear differently."* Teachers should know how to secure the classroom and what their options are if not in a safe location. In these situations, it is the calmness and reassurance of the teacher that matters.

Family:

- I turned my phone off so I could take care of the students. When I turned my phone back on there were 14 messages from my mother telling me to call my kids because they were afraid I was the one that was dead.
- My daughter teaches at another school and they released her so she could come check on me.
- My husband called and said, "I'm coming to get you."
- I have to be brave for my family. They don't want me to come back to the school.
- I had 15 calls from people wanting to know if I was okay.

Reaction

Lesson

Lesson: In today's world of instant messaging, all staff should be reminded and given time, once all are safe, to call or text family members to let them know they are safe and will be home after making sure that their students' needs are met.

Family is family. In a crisis, family members need to know, as quickly as possible, that their loved ones are safe. Many students contact parents immediately. However, because staff were so focused on the well-being of their students, they were not thinking about the need to reassure their own family members.

The Killing of a Beloved Coach

In May of 2008, an EF5 tornado struck Parkersburg, Iowa. Seven died, 70 people were injured and 400 homes were destroyed. For this small community the losses seemed overwhelming. Ed Thomas, a well-known high school football coach, who had several of his players playing in the NFL, led the community recovery efforts. It was his spirit, faith and leadership that led to the rebuilding of the community physically and spiritually. In June of 2010, Coach Thomas was tragically shot and killed in front of 24 students he was meeting with that day. The community was again devastated at the loss of their leader.

The Thomas family encouraged them not to forget his spirit and faith and demonstrated their faith by embracing the Becker family, whose son had killed the coach, knowing that they too had fought hard to help their son with his mental illness. Ed Thomas was actually honored when his family was presented with the Arthur Ashe Award for Courage at the 2010 ESPY awards ceremony. Also in 2010 the Ed Thomas Law was made effective, requiring police notification when a psychiatric patient with pending legal action was to be released. The Beckers's son was released from a psychiatric facility the day before the killing; police were not notified.

Approximately one year following the murder, I was asked to meet with the parents of the students who had witnessed his death. At the end of the school day I was also asked to talk with the entire staff. I supported their resilience, strength, their faith and forgiveness. I normalized those reactions that I had learned from previous experience others are likely still carrying with them even one year later. My intuitive sense was that individuals were hesitant to share anything that might contradict the outgoing spirit of the community. This was confirmed when two individuals very briefly indicated to me after the presentation that there were a number people in pain and struggling with all that had happened the past two years, despite the resilience and faith displayed by the larger community. This was also confirmed later in the evening when meeting with the parents.

What stands out most in my mind about that evening is that parents talked as if this just happened several days ago. Despite the support, generosity and faith of the community, their worries and reactions remained troublesome. They worried about the long-term impact this would have on their children. They indicated they had received no formal debriefing or intervention other than the first time they came together as a group shortly after the murder. Parents also indicated that they felt they were having a harder time adjusting than their own children. **The resilience of this community has**

been remarkable. Other communities faced with similar tragedies have not done as well. And yet, just as there is no one intervention that fits everyone's needs, there is no single community response that heals all its members.

Reaction

Lesson

Lesson: This experience focuses on the parents of the students whose children were witnesses to the murder of their beloved coach. It reminds us that just as professionals are vulnerable to compassion fatigue and vicarious trauma, so too are parents. Still, I have found over the years that schools provide limited help to parents following a crisis their children have experienced. This makes no sense. As parents struggle they find it difficult to meet their children's needs. This increases their children's worries and anxieties. Children in this situation will spend far less time with their parents and at home. They become overwhelmed and frightened by their parents' struggles. If this continues for any length of time, school performance suffers and challenging behaviors emerge.

Schools themselves are not therapeutic environments. However, it seems reasonable, after a school related crisis, that the school social workers, counselors or psychologists trained in crisis intervention and short-term trauma-focused support ought to be assigned to help the parents of the children most exposed. This provides both parents and students easier accesses to help and allows parents, students, teachers and social workers the opportunity to work together in a coordinated effort to restore the stability of all involved, especially the children.

I understand that this approach may be difficult for many schools, even though it may be the most effective way of helping the most-exposed families and facilitating those students' ongoing success in school. **From a trauma-informed perspective, this issue is the very reason that communities are urged to initiate a trauma-informed task force consisting of the major mental health facilities, child and family care providers in the communities whose staff are committed to working interactively with schools where children are most accessible. In such a network all would have the same training so they are on the *same page* as to the needs of those who are in crisis or in trauma. This trauma-informed group of community professionals can then be called upon to work with students and their parents when school staff cannot do so directly.**

The Unexpected

Years ago a 6-year-old shot and killed another 6-year-old in school. As unimaginable as this may sound, a review of the history of violence in that child's family and the easy access to guns in the home made it not surprising. The school had no formal crisis team so it relied upon community mental health professionals and school district social workers for help.

There was worldwide media coverage. Their satellite trucks blocked the surrounding neighboring streets to residential traffic. Equipped with telephoto lenses, some camera crews set up in the backyards of the homes facing the school in attempts to get photos of students and staff. It was quite intrusive for everyone. People reported that the beating blades of the hovering helicopters were *thunderous* and frightened the children. As to be expected, many of the early news reports were inaccurate, intensifying reactions and fueling wild assumptions.

I received a call to assist the primary responders approximately two weeks later. I recommended the 40 some members of this group be placed into smaller groups so each would have time to process the many thoughts, reactions and challenges they faced helping the students and staff with whom they had direct contact with in the days that followed. I also wanted to be sure to group the most-exposed responders together, so as not to further activate those who had limited exposure as direct witnesses. However, the administrator indicated that the only opportunity to meet with these individuals was to meet with all of them at one time. This made a formal intervention quite impossible. Believing that some intervention is better than no intervention following traumatic situations, I presented only five questions, staying away from those related to exposure details and feelings.

The intervention itself went well. During my summary I normalized the many thoughts and reactions they had shared, prepared them for reactions they may still have in the weeks and months to come and presented them with a number of ways to help them with the self-care they needed after the intense exposure they had experienced. I then provided them with contact information should any of them wish to have additional assistance. As participants stood up to leave, to everyone's surprise including myself, the administrator arrived with a professional photographer announcing he wanted to take a picture of everyone in the group and provide them copies as a way to remember the help that they provided the children and his staff. Not a sound could be heard. Many faces were frozen in disbelief. Why would anyone want a picture associated with the tragic and violent death of a child by another child? It was not an occasion to celebrate. For what was likely just a few seconds no one moved. At that point I quickly spoke up and indicated everyone was free to go. Some stayed, many did not.

Reaction

Lesson

Lesson: In this situation, attempting to help 40 primary responders who included mental health workers, social workers and school staff was challenging due to restrictions and cautions. The first question this situation raised was whether an intervention under these conditions should be attempted. If so, how would it be structured, what would be its purpose? My experiences working in crisis walk-in centers and suicide prevention/intervention programs and providing intervention to victims of violence (involving physical and sexual assault, domestic violence and murder) has taught me a valuable lesson about working with those in highly emotional states—unable to think clearly or manage their reactions. **It was always my experience that some intervention was better than no intervention. However, for the intervention to be the most helpful, it had to be directed at helping those in crisis achieve some degree of stabilization (self-regulation) in their immediate lives. To achieve this, in ways those in crisis felt safe to engage, the intervention process needed to be explained and accepted by the participants. It also needed to be structured, its objectives supportive of stabilization efforts and adhered to by those providing the intervention.**

One of the primary objectives of this intervention was to help participants discover that, despite their varied training and levels of expertise, they were all experiencing many of the same thoughts and reactions, which were quite normal given what they experienced. Normalization of these reactions was critical as well as discovering they were not alone in what they were experiencing. Other objectives were to educate them as to what to expect in the days and weeks that followed and suggest several ways to help manage their stress. The final objective was to be realistic as to what the intervention could and could not accomplish. Contact information needed to be available for anyone who wished to have additional assistance beyond this intervention. These objectives were accomplished.

In order to achieve these objectives, the introduction of the intervention to the participants was critical. The introduction needed to establish group expectations, how the process would work and how confidentiality would be maintained. Following is the introduction presented to this group.

> *Intervention for primary responders, following such tragic incidents, is best done in small groups of no more than eight participants in each group so each of you have the opportunity to process the many thoughts and reactions situations like this can induce even in the most experienced professional. Obviously this was not possible for your group, so contact information will be provided should you wish additional assistance. Some intervention is better than no intervention and this intervention will bring some relief and normalcy to all that you have experienced. We will only ask five questions and allow time for as many responses as you wish to provide. There is no need for us to respond to your comments; we and you can simply listen to what others have to say. As you listen, I think you'll find that you share similar reactions, that you are*

not alone with your reactions and that all you have experienced is not at all unusual. Before we conclude, a summary of all that was learned will be given along with suggestions for helping with the reactions you may continue to experience. Recovering from this kind of experience takes time. You will find some relief today but it will take time. The intervention will go no longer than two hours. No notes will be taken to maintain confidentiality and we expect that you will respect what others say by not discussing what is said here today with others outside of this group.

One last note, some of you were more exposed to all that happened than others. Normally, we would meet with the most exposed in your own group. Since this is not possible, we will avoid asking questions about the details of what may have been witnessed by some of you who were at the scene immediately. Again, should any of you wish further assistance following this intervention, contact information is available. This having been said, let's begin with the initial question.

The Critical Questions

The questions presented were critical to protecting the emotional safety of all involved. At the same time they allowed participants to respond in detail as to their many reactions in order for all members to learn they shared similar reactions. To save time, participants were asked to identify who they were and what their role was in this crisis if they chose to answer any one of the questions presented. The first question asked was, "What one thought stands out the most for you since this happened?" This question kept the focus on their thoughts versus their emotions. It was a safe question for most to answer and set the stage for those who were initially reluctant to participate (as reported by participants before leaving).

When asked, "What was the worst part?" participants identified events following the incident such as the funeral, the media issues, community member and parent reactions; specific factors reminding them of what happened and difficulties they experienced in trying to help the most exposed. For example, I remember several of the mental health professionals telling how they planned to spend time asking the children specific questions and how all that fell apart in the first five minutes because the children were not ready to sit quietly for an orderly discussion. "We did the best we could," they said, "but we weren't trained to work with younger children in crisis. We ended up just letting them play."

Reaction

Lesson

Lesson: Obviously, having a developmental understanding of the needs of those in crisis is essential to providing a beneficial intervention. However, in numerous situations in years that followed, it was not unusual to hear how members of high school crisis teams were sent to assist elementary students in crisis only to realize they did not have the skills or resources needed to help at that developmental level. **It is always easier to send elementary staff to assist at the high school level, where cognitive approaches are more developmentally appropriate, than to send high school staff to assist elementary-aged children where sensory-based, nontalking interventions are more appropriate.**

When asked, "Of all the thoughts or reactions you had, what one reaction or thought surprised you the most?" participants detailed more personal reactions—for example, disbelief, denial, not being able to think clearly, being numb, confused, moving in slow motion, freezing, and not being able to perform simple tasks such as dialing frequently called phone numbers. Several talked about how difficult it was for them to get past the disbelief that this young child had actually shot and killed a peer. This question allowed some of the participants who had not previously responded to now express themselves. The next question of "Where are you experiencing this the most in your body?" further helped to build a "shared connectedness" among participants, as each could easily state their physical response to all that happened. Those unable to identify earlier reactions could now also state the physical reactions they were experiencing. This helped develop a sense of normalcy and "connectedness" with one another. The final question, "What have you learned from this?" evoked a number of responses regarding the need for training and developing of school protocols.

Following this process, the summary normalized the many reactions presented by the group. It supported that reactions may continue as it takes time to recover from such tragic situations; but, that this recovery had begun with this intervention. They were all supported for all they had done for the children and staff involved, even though for many this was not a situation they had been prepared to manage or even anticipated would be a possibility.

Lesson: For a group intervention to be safe and beneficial for those in crisis, it is critical that the expectations of the intervention are clearly presented, that it has achievable appropriate objectives, which are guided by specifically structured questions that allow participants to reveal their many varied thoughts and reactions in a safe manner. In addition, those leading such an intervention must be prepared for the unexpected and be prepared to remind participants of the choices they have available to them if whatever is happening does not feel safe for them.

Safely Helping Those in Crisis

When learning to debrief (a process no longer supported by the National Institute for Mental Health [NIMH]), I remember sitting in on two debriefing sessions as an observer. Participants were mandated to attend these groups. In each group there was a participant who was extremely emotional. The debriefer, a highly recommended professional, did little to limit what each of these individuals was expressing and actually used reflection and a series of questions that encouraged extensive emoting. In one group, one individual's lengthy responses, which were allowed and encouraged by the debriefer, consumed a good 45 minutes in this two-hour session. In the other group, another individual's responses consumed almost a full hour of the process. This significantly limited the attention given to the other participants, who I'm sure felt, as I did, that this was not only not helpful, but, in fact, created more stress for all involved.

These two highly emotionally charged meetings left everyone uncomfortable. The vulnerable individuals, who were encouraged to process their feelings, were put at risk in an intervention that was designed to be a brief, educational, supportive, single session intervention. I'm sure the two highly emotional individuals who were required to attend these sessions were left feeling they had expressed far too much, to the point of worrying what their colleagues now thought about them. Their colleagues, who attended in hopes of finding some relief for themselves, were left with more stress as a result of being exposed to these highly emotional processes.

Reaction

Lesson

Lesson: There is a time when some individuals do need help exploring and processing their emotional reactions. If one understands the needs of those in crisis, doing so when in crisis and in a group setting with peers is not the time. What they need most is to discover that what they are experiencing is not unusual, that they can regulate those reactions even for short periods of time, that listening to others can be extremely helpful in discovering that they are not alone with their reactions and that appreciating each other as survivors brings a sense of comfort and hope. It was these two experiences that led me to developing a process that was not mandatory and would not allow for the processing of feelings.

In essence the earlier lesson about crisis intervention being structured, with very clear objectives and supportive processes, was used to develop a process that prevented this supportive and valuable intervention from becoming more like a therapeutic process. In the ideal world, potential participants can be screened, so the highly emotional and most-exposed participants could be screened and either be seen in their own group or individually. However, this was not always possible, making it imperative to regulate the responses of those highly emotional, most exposed individuals from becoming the focus of attention. In so doing, it taught them they could experience relief without having to explore or process their feelings. This did not preclude suggesting to some of the participants, following these sessions, that additional short-term assistance outside of the school setting might be beneficial.

I trained thousands of school social workers, counselors, social workers and mental health professionals over the past 20 years in this process. Consider that counselors and mental health professionals are trained to be reflective, to explore and process feelings—not to sit quietly. It is difficult for them to resist the urge to reflect or make comments about each individual's responses because it feels as if they are ignoring the participants by not sharing their insight. Although some survivors might need help processing their emotional reactions in the days to come, it is initially difficult for professionals to accept that processing feelings is not initially necessary for relief and can serve to actually further exacerbate the reactions survivors are experiencing. It is difficult for them to accept that what they might say in response to participant's responses can actually get in the way of healing. It is difficult for them to trust that healing is taking place as survivors listen to each other describe their different responses.

Although professionals I have trained have always appreciated the need for a structured approach when working with those in crisis, changing their mindsets regarding the processing of emotions was difficult. It demanded dramatic demonstrations involving examples that actually took place in school settings. I used two actual situations: The one was the killing of a superintendent by an employee; the other was the sudden death of a staff person while in the teacher's lounge.

The participants were given a few of the responses actually given by those who were involved in these situations. In the initial role-play, three professionals were given no preparation other than to use their counseling skills. They were given a brief summary of what had happened and a few minutes to decide how they would begin. The initial role-play demonstrated what happens when typical counseling skills are used, when the process is unstructured and when individuals are allowed to provide more information than is asked for at the time. It is especially dangerous when they are encouraged to move into their emotional reactions with the use of reflection or statements like, "Tell me more."

Prior to the second role-play, the same intervenors from the first role-play, who had relied upon counseling skills only to lose control of the group, were instructed in the more appropriate process. In the hundreds of demonstrations conducted, the intervenors and participants alike found the second role-play to be far safer. Participants indicated that they found what the other participants had to say was more important and the process less disruptive than when the intervenors were reacting to their responses in the initial role-play.

Wildfire: An Unexpected Delay in Recovery

In 2011 Texas experienced the worst wildfire in its history in Bastrop, Texas. The first call to 911 came at 2:20pm on September 4; by 4pm Bastrop Middle

School became a temporary shelter. This fire covered over 34,356 acres and left 1,645 families homeless; 486 students and 80 employees lost their homes to the fire. Hundreds of students became homeless, adding to their trauma. Because the evacuation of the city was so quick people were unable to take anything with them. Many of their pets died. School counselors, social workers and teachers, some of whom also lost their homes, spent the entire school year providing support to students as well as to one another as best they could. A few years earlier I assisted a number of these counselors and social workers with the development of their crisis team recovery protocol and interventions. They indicated that these protocol and interventions gave them the structure and direction they needed to help minimize what was an overwhelming situation for everyone.

About one year following this fire they asked me to return to review the work they had done and to offer additional suggestions. They had faced many issues in the previous year that their plan had not considered. Children were being shuttled from one family to another, from one shelter to another. Families were staying in homes with other families, adding stress not only to the homeless families, but also to the families who generously took in those homeless families. Hotels were occupied for months. A number of families whose homes were not totally destroyed were kept from returning to them for months because insurance companies took time processing their claims.

School buses were rerouted to pick up students from the hotels. Staff faced one challenge after another. School counselors could never get away from dealing with the mental health issues associated with the fire. Keep in mind that 80 staff had also been displaced. Both students and staff exhibited the reactions of post-traumatic stress disorder (PTSD). As early as 1987, McFarland, Policansky and Irwin (1987) reported high levels of trauma 8 and 21 months following a massive fire. The Texas fire was massive and destructive and the trauma- and grief-related reactions experienced by the members of that community were pervasive. The District Team did an excellent job attending to the basic needs of those most impacted by the fire. They also did an excellent job meeting their mental health needs. However, what was never anticipated was the duration of help that would be needed because of the prolonged homelessness of so many.

What added to the stress and compassion fatigue among staff was the 10-month delay in recovery efforts to rebuild the community. That delay intensified and prolonged the trauma and grief experienced by so many families because of the visual memories of the fire they could not escape. It induced tremendous stress in the school staff as they were being reminded every day of the impact this was having on their students. What was unbelievable is that the Brown Toad, an endangered species that inhabited the area, became the source of this delay. It was actually the Endangered Species Act that prohibited FEMA from beginning its work to remove all of the debris so the community could be rebuilt and families could return. The political nonsense that took place between FEMA and the administrators of the Endangered Species Act over this 10-month period was beyond shameful. To think that the interest of a toad would come before the well-being of hundreds of families is unforgiveable. "Expect the unexpected" is more than an understatement in this case.

Reaction

Lesson

Lesson: Given the changing ecological conditions of our planet, weather patterns are likely to bring greater disasters. Contingency planning with neighboring school districts and counties that may be required to absorb large numbers of students, as was the case in Houston, is especially critical. Contingency disaster planning is critical to minimizing extended trauma. In this case, mental health needs were great but even greater was providing and sustaining resources for meeting basic needs. In many ways, the entire community had to rebuild their lives all over.

When Organizations Are Not Trauma-Informed

In the early 1970s I was working at a walk-in crisis center in an area that had three major psychiatric facilities for children and adults. Seventy percent of the walk-ins had psychiatric histories while the others were in crisis because of issues ranging from divorce and depression to exposure to violence. While working at this program, one of the staff nurses took her life. This was a shock to all of us who had spent many hours working together with her on client problems. The next morning a meeting was called. We were asked how we were doing, nothing more. A few words were said that I cannot remember and then we were back at work. As we all know, the suicide of a friend or colleague can be very emotionally challenging and raise a lot of self-doubt and many "What if?" questions. This was never approached. The message was fairly clear: As professionals we should be able to manage our reactions and, if we cannot, then we need to question our value as a professional. After that meeting no one spoke openly about what happened, nor was it brought up in subsequent meetings.

I remember several staff from a local mental health program struggling with what they had experienced two weeks earlier. While on a day trip a client had died accidentally while in their presence. It was decided by the administration to offer a debriefing at the end of day, as staff needed to be with clients during the day. Most brought their lunches to the table, which raised an immediate red flag related to the self-care of these professionals, as well as the level of organizational awareness as to the needs of its staff when exposed to what was a very traumatic experience. They were clearly exhausted. In the two weeks prior, they had been interviewed by police and were vulnerable to numerous articles appearing in the local papers that were critical of mental health and questioning staff accountability. When I asked them what the past two weeks had been like, they indicated that everyday had been nonstop in terms of caring for clients and that this was the first time they had been provided time for themselves.

Reaction

Lesson

Lesson: First responders are vulnerable to vicarious trauma. Unfortunately, the care needed by first responders is often forgotten or not attended to because of limited resources to assist them, or because they get lost in the demands of work that has gone unattended because of the crisis. The need for self-care strategies has been mentioned several times as has the creation of a community-wide trauma-informed task force that would have the resources available to support primary responders.

Crisis Team/Responder Issues

The experiences previously presented also address several issues related to crisis teams, their interventions, preparedness and responsibility and the ongoing learning that helps improve the quality of their responses. These are discussed briefly before presenting the additional experiences of survivors.

Not every crisis is traumatic, but every trauma induces crisis in its survivors. In either case, crisis intervention should be the initial intervention of choice as it involves actions that frame Psychological First Aid (PFA). It also goes further in helping those in crisis stabilize and then manage the reactions induced by a crisis. However, in trainings, participants are consistently unable to identify specific questions that help survivors manage their emotions, make meaning of what has happened, take action, and find resolution—all key components of crisis intervention (Echterling & Presbury, 2005). For example, I will ask attendees to identify one question they might ask a person in crisis that would let them know whether that person can think beyond the crisis. Very few can. I might ask them to identify one question that would help that person realize he/she has the inner resource to manage. Very few can. I might ask them to compose several statements they would want to present the person in crisis that would emphasize their resilience and ability to manage now and in the future. They struggle to compose a script.

Reaction

> **Lesson**
>
>
>

Lesson: In crisis situations what we say and what we ask are critical to effectively helping survivors stabilize, manage, and discover their inner strength and resilience. As crisis team members, we ought to be proficient in providing crisis intervention and know all the possibilities of how we might respond and act before entering that crisis. This can be prepared far in advance of crises happening.

Following Protocol

I remember being asked to testify on a family's behalf in a lawsuit claiming the school had induced PTSD in their child by the intervention provided their child following a traumatic incident at that school. The parents had clearly indicated that they did not want their child involved in the school's intervention. Unfortunately that request was never communicated to the social workers providing intervention. Based on family history, I concluded the intervention itself did not induce PTSD in their child although it certainly intensified the anxiety existing prior to the school incident. The school's communication failure clearly led to the inclusion of this child in an intervention the parents had stated they did not want for their child. The schools failure to follow the parents' wishes did leave them legally vulnerable.

> **Reaction**
>
>
>

> **Lesson**
>
>
>
>

**Lesson: Legal counsel should review all protocol for possible vul-
nerability to litigation. Once approved, one of the responsibilities of a
crisis team member is to monitor team responses to ensure they are following protocol, especially when members from other teams are asked
to assist.**

Being Prepared

Neuroscience clearly documents that those experiencing extreme stress, crises and or trauma are often overwhelmed by midbrain response-feelings,
physiological and biological reactions, and difficulty thinking, hearing what
is being said and processing what has happened. Crisis team responders are
especially vulnerable to these same reactions when they fail to prepare themselves before entering into that crisis situation. I am continually surprised by
how many school crisis team members do not keep a copy of their protocol
in their cars, understanding that they may not have access to them in the facility in the midst of a crisis. Reviewing them before going into a crisis benefits
them as well as those they are about to help.

Fire and police consistently train and practice responses for various situations in addition to actually intervening in these situations regularly. Their
cognitive brains regulate their emotional, nervous system responses so they
do not interfere with what must be done quickly and decisively. The reality is
that crises do not happen every week or even every month in school settings
so it's very easy to be overwhelmed and to forget those intervention strategies
and recovery tasks. Being able to quickly turn to the page / section in the crisis
team manual and review the tasks and intervention strategies specific to that
situation engages the thinking brain. This begins to help regulate the anxiety
normal in these situations and leave responders a little less vulnerable when
walking into what can be challenging reactions and behaviors from students
and staff. In addition, the role of a crisis team demands that its members are
organized and quickly engage the tasks outlined in their crisis manual. This
is simply difficult to do without immediate access to that manual and its incident specific responses.

Reaction

Lesson

Lesson: Be prepared with immediate accessibility to valuable resources and prepare yourself before entering that crisis.

Teachable Moments Lost

There have been a number of occasions when I have spent a day with all the crisis team members of a district to address recovery protocols and interventions. In an effort to learn more about their experiences, what they have and have not done immediately following a crisis, I'll ask them to think about one of the experiences they directly responded to and what they were least prepared for at the time that they engaged the victims and survivors in that situation. As their stories unfold, other team members may have been aware of that incident, but not at all aware of what their colleagues had to face in that situation, what they did or did not do, what went well and what did not go well.

As more begin to share their experiences and what they were least prepared for, the group discovers that others among them faced similar experiences and that they could have been a wonderful resource at the time. They also begin teaching one another various ways to respond in a crisis, discover protocols they have questions about, scenarios they had not thought about, additional resources that would be helpful, and sections of their protocols that needed revising. This exercise is a wonderfully enriching, teachable moment for everyone as it helps to identify their areas of competence as well as areas needing attention. Unfortunately, this kind of processing rarely happens. It is not unusual for district-wide team members to go two years without meeting as a group to simply share their experiences with each other in a structured learning process.

Reaction

Lesson

Lesson: District-wide teams who do not come together at least once a year to share all they have experienced are not learning to be better prepared, more effective and efficient in their responses. When these teachable moments are lost, the valuable lessons they teach are lost.

Survivors of Suicide

The individual responses of nonfatal suicide attempters and the surviving siblings and parents of murdered siblings, sons and daughters are presented. Given that suicide and homicide rates of young people remain at epidemic levels, it is important that crisis team members be prepared to respond to these survivors.

Nonfatal Suicide Attempters

Following are a number of statements made directly to me by nonfatal attempters. See if you can identify the issue being addressed and the lessons these statements teach us.

- I'm no prize.
- No one really cares.
- I'm just a burden to everyone.
- I can't do anything right.
- It's always going to be this way. It's never going to change.
- It's their way or no way.
- Even if I do what they want, it's never good enough. I just can't win.
- I'll never be what they want me to be.
- My feelings don't mean anything. It's like I don't exist.
- If I kill myself, they'll change.

Reaction

Lesson

Lesson: These are the voices of nonfatal suicide attempters and their thoughts. They indicated these thoughts repeatedly occupied their lives prior to their attempts. They reflect reality, but also distortions about themselves, others and the future. They also reflect attachment issues with parents. It can be argued, in some cases, when biological factors are not a dominant factor, that suicide is induced by early and repeated traumatic interactions with parents. These leave children feeling powerless, hopeless, a failure in the eyes of their parents, alone and without a meaningful sense of attachment. Many of the nonfatal attempters I have met, when asked, indicated that prior to their nonfatal attempt that they had no significant connection to an adult in their lives.

Using positive verbal responses to reframe their thoughts not only frequently failed but, at times, led to a long list of negative, "yes, but" replies. This is when I realized that their thoughts were likely shaped by their experiences at home, which would be impossible to change in the short time we would be meeting. I believed the only way to move them to a different way of thinking was to involve them in experiences that resulted in strength-based, resilient focused thoughts about self, others and their future. I discovered that actions and interactions with suicidal youth can be far more effective than talk therapy; although, at some point, effort is needed to make them aware of the distortions in the way they thought about themselves and others. This will be discussed shortly. It was one family in particular that taught me the importance of taking action with potentially suicidal individuals.

I spent months meeting with a struggling family whose teenage son had been expressing suicidal thoughts that seemed to fall on deaf ears.

The father worked two jobs. Not only did the father have little influence in home life, but the son saw him as weak and helpless in the face of the domineering mother. One day the son had his last fight with his mother, who basically expressed her disappointment and shame about him. She told him, "Don't bother talking to me until you are ready to do what I know is best for you." As he left the house he said to his younger brother, "No one will ever have to worry about me again." He was fully intent on ending his life that day.

His father arrived home perhaps 20 minutes after his son had left the house. When the younger brother told his father what happened and what his older brother said, the father immediately got in the car to find his son. Approximately 30 minutes later, the father found him walking alone. He stopped the car, got out and maneuvered his son into the car. Every day for the following three weeks he took his son with him to his workplace after school. The son reported to me months later that it was this one action by his father that helped him the most. It did not resolve all his issues, but it changed the way he thought about himself and his father. He said his father still wasn't around much, but at least he knew he cared and would do what he could to help him. He said, "I didn't think he cared before because we never did anything together."

It wasn't until years later I came across Alfred Adler's (1930) concept of *private logic*. Private logic refers to the thoughts that are shaped by our experiences and that ultimately drive our behaviors. It was this father's one action that changed his son's thoughts and ultimately his behavior when confronted with other stressful situations.

Reaction

Lesson

Lesson: If we want children to be resilient, we need to engage them in experiences that induce strength-based thoughts about self, others and life. Trying to do this initially with suicidal youth using verbal efforts would be difficult.

Potentially Suicidal Thoughts

The aforementioned thoughts that occupied the minds of those who did attempt suicide can be used to connect with suicidal youth in a way that momentarily allows them to see you as someone who has some sense of what their world has been like. I learned quickly that, rather than trying to counter or reframe their thoughts, if I simply presented what I knew their thoughts were likely to be, they connected much quicker with me as someone who perhaps understood their world. It opened the door for me to take the simplest of actions to let them know, without words, that I was not like their parents and did see them as having value. I always began presenting these thoughts with, "I wouldn't be surprised if you have thought to yourself . . ."

Lesson: Having knowledge of the thought processes that occupy the lives of potentially suicidal individuals provides the opportunity to connect with those individuals by acknowledging our awareness of the thoughts they are likely having or had at some point.

"If I Kill Myself, They'll Change"

This one statement, "If I kill myself, they'll change," is a distorted thought that shows how suicidal individuals are not focused on the permanency of what they are about to do, but on getting something they have long desired. Often, when I asked potentially suicidal youth what would change if they did this, they would respond in present tense, as if they would be there to enjoy the change.

I remember one teen telling me he was going to kill himself on his father's birthday. When I use this example in training, I asked participants what they might say in response. Most reply with a question such as, "When is your father's birthday?" Obviously we need to know this, but it does not help make a connection with this teen. When I again ask participants what they might say, not ask this teen, the room goes quiet. A few brave souls will take a chance but usually frame their statement in a question such as, "You must really be mad at your dad?" When asking them what it is that this teen needs to hear, people struggle because they don't understand that this teen, like so many others, is not focused on dying but on his need for something to change. This teen needed to be made aware of the problem with his thinking. The statement I actually made to this teen was, *"It sounds as if your dad hurt you and disappointed you one too many times and you want to hurt him back. This makes sense. What does not make sense is that if you do this you will be dead and unable to see his reaction. If you want to hurt your dad, let him know he can't keep doing this to you without you fighting back, there are things you can do and be around to see the result."*

What this statement did was help the individual focus on the fact that what he wanted is for something to change, not to die in the process. When I then asked him what his dad did or did not do that caused him to get to this point, he rattled off a list of behaviors and disappointments. At this point, the connection between us was made and over time he made great progress.

Reaction

Lesson

Lesson: Listening and helping potentially suicidal youth focus on the fact they are not wanting to die, but instead wanting something or someone in their lives to change, can help to shift their thought process to more appropriate problem solving. Suicidal individuals are overwhelmed and driven by their thoughts, whereas traumatized individuals are overwhelmed and driven more by their emotional and physical reactions, sensations and images of what happened.

Surviving Siblings

Surviving siblings often experience the following thoughts:

- It's like others are afraid of me now.
- Nobody wants to talk about it.
- My parents are all broken up. He ruined our life.
- One day my parents were there and now, since this happened, it's like they're gone and I'm invisible.
- I can't say anything bad about my brother, how he blamed me for stuff he did. They think he was perfect.
- I'll never be as good as they make him now.

Reaction

Lesson

Lesson: These thoughts of surviving siblings reflect the disrupted parental attachment that is frequently experienced by surviving siblings as well as the distancing from peers, who no longer know what to think about them or what to say. Such disengagement places surviving siblings at risk. When a sibling ends his or her life, surviving siblings can be placed at risk due to the alienation, emotional abandonment and the judgmental responses they can experience from parents and peers alike. The behaviors of the surviving siblings, under these conditions, can change significantly. They often include behaviors and actions that call attention to them, but in negative ways, especially from those who do not understand the ways the sibling's world has been shattered by suicide.

When Their Suicide Attempts Failed

I remember a number of students and their nonfatal suicide attempts. Mandy, who was 15, stated that she was generally a pretty optimistic person until a series of losses and major changes in a time span of just a few months led to her attempt. Her mother went through a difficult divorce. Following the divorce, they needed to relocate, which meant Mandy lost contact with some of her friends and had to adjust to a new school and make new friends. Money was tight, which further limited Mandy's activities and options.

One day, after a fight with her father, she stayed home from school and took an overdose. It was interesting to note that before she passed out, she called her boyfriend who lived across town. She never indicated, while on the phone, that she had taken an overdose. He sensed something was wrong and called Mandy's mother. Her mother was only several blocks away at work. When he told her that Mandy was home and not in school and that she didn't sound right, her mother left work immediately. When she drove up the driveway, she saw Mandy lying on the porch unconscious. Emergency medical services rushed her to the hospital. After they pumped her stomach they told her mother that if another 5 minutes had passed Mandy would have died. When I asked Mandy what her first thought was when she woke up, she said, "I'm glad I didn't die."

Alecia, age 16, had a much different response. After her first attempt at stabbing herself to death failed, I asked her what her first thought was when she awoke. She said, "I was mad I didn't die." She later succeeded at ending her life while Mandy went on to flourish.

Reaction

Lesson

Lesson: School social workers often ask how they can be assured that nonfatal attempters will not attempt again. Actually **there is no absolute assurance when dealing with those who have already attempted that they will not attempt again.** So much can take place in such a short period of time. We have little control over what may subsequently lead to that additional attempt. **However, Mandy and Alecia's first response following their failed attempt gives us one predictor as to their available strength or vulnerability.** Mandy's response was one of relief and hope. Alecia's response was one of frustration and despair. However, hope can quickly vanish in the face of another crisis and despair can become deadly. **Helping nonfatal attempters develop areas of competence to enhance their sense of worth and esteem is essential to their resilience in the face of crises they will continue to encounter in their young lives.** Schools provide multiple opportunities through academics and extracurricular programs for students to develop areas of competence. **Keep in mind, it is the action we take to help them that matters the most in bringing about changes in the way they think about themselves and life.**

After Suicide

I remember assisting numerous schools across the country following student suicide by encouraging them to go into the classrooms and talk to the students about suicide in an informational way. I suggested discussing what they can say to their friends who might be thinking about it and what they can do. (This classroom presentation and the most common questions students ask about suicide and recommended answers can be found in *Interventions Following Suicide and Other Traumatic Losses,* [Steele, 2005].) I also remember being asked to return by several of these schools following additional suicides and attempts. In every case, when I asked if they had met with the students in class following the initial suicide the answer was "No."

Reaction

Lesson

Lesson: In the previous father-son experience the lesson learned was the importance of taking action. **Failure to meet with students following the suicide of another student is failure to take action. It is essentially ignoring their need for attention following an experience that can leave them with many questions and fears. The absence of this attention fuels their sense of alienation from the adult world and leaves them feeling that adults really do not care. Unfortunately, the vulnerable youth are also left to think, "I guess it's going to take a few more suicides before they decide to take us seriously." The logic makes sense to them and they will take action.**

Survivors of Homicide

Following are the voices of children who were the survivors of homicide.

- Sometimes in school when I'm doing my work I can still see my friend lying there.
- I dream he's calling me to help him but I can't. I can't get to him. I can't help him.
- I watch where I walk now.
- I'm going to get a gun and blow off the head of the person who did this to my brother.
- I was at my friend's house when she was shot through the window. It's been a year and I still jump when there are loud noises.
- I wonder when it's going to be me.

Reaction

Lesson

Lesson: These statements reflect the intrusive memories, startle responses, fear, sense of hopelessness, revenge and a constantly terrifying readiness for trauma to happen again not only to others but also to themselves. They also tell us the body remembers the many sensations and sensory elements (sounds, sights, smells, touch) it was exposed to in traumatic situations. The reactions experienced can then be activated in the present when similar sensory elements associated with what happened occur in the present. This is why any intervention with traumatized students needs to include a variety of self-regulation activities that can be easily learned and used as needed. This is important for learning because as long as victims are activated or in the state of arousal, that intense anxiety makes it far more difficult to focus, retain, recall and make sense of what is being communicated.

Children exposed to violence experience unthinkable emotional burdens that definitely impact learning and behavior when trauma-specific intervention is not provided. The Center for Disease Control and Prevention ACE study (2011) that examined the events traumatized youth experienced over many years definitively supports the long-term negative impact of trauma when not attended to in the early years. This further supports the need for schools to be trauma-informed and to provide evidence-based school interventions to assist the growing number of today's students in trauma. It makes sense for this to be provided because this is where students are most accessible for help. These practices can be easily integrated into the curriculum to benefit the entire student body and staff. The fact is when we fail to give children the opportunities to bring us into their world we cannot discover what they have or have not been experiencing. How can we then possibly know what will be most helpful to them? We cannot.

Adult Survivors

As a few of the previous experiences revealed, staff are just as vulnerable to trauma-specific reactions as are the children in their care. Exposure to trauma can decrease their effectiveness in the classroom as well as negatively impact relationships with their peers. It can also make it difficult for some to continue working in the environment where the trauma took place. Following the December 14, 2012 mass killings at Sandy Hook Elementary School, a number of staff resigned even though the students and staff were moved to another school. For some, just being in the presence of those students was a constant reminder of all that happened, how they themselves acted during that horrible day, the "should haves" and "could haves" and other memories they carried with them in silence.

As indicated in the Oklahoma experience, the physical reminders for some needed to be avoided in order to best cope. The following stories from adult survivors give us a view of the thoughts, memories and reactions any adult can experience, whether they are professionals caring for children or responding to traumatic incidents. Their stories also teach us invaluable lessons to support the way we assist adults exposed to trauma.

A Sister's Response

I remember spending time with an adult sister whose brother was shot and killed. She described when she ran up to his body. She was afraid to touch him and heard herself thinking, "If I touch him he will die."

Reaction

Lesson

Lesson: Whatever children experience in trauma, adults can experience as well. This sister's response involved magical thinking, generally expressed by younger children. This teaches us that school staff are not immune to

the reactions of their students following traumatic incidents. They too need attending in the same way we attend to children following trauma.

A Mother's Daughter

I remember a mother whose daughter was shot and killed. I spent hours with her. Following all that time that I spent with her, the words I remember most were, "when you lose a parent you lose a part of your past, but when you lose a child you lose your future." Although this was 23 years ago, I can still hear her voice as if she's talking to me now. This loss was especially difficult for the surviving sister, who not only lost her best friend but now her mother to the many reactions she experienced following the murder. Fortunately, a number of friends helped her join a Parents of Murdered Children support group (POMC). It took time, but her resilience emerged and her gratitude led her to form a POMC support group in her area.

Reaction

Lesson

Lesson: This mother's story indicates that, with a little help, those who suffer incredibly painful losses can discover their resilience and do for others what others have done for them.

A Father's Son

I remember being with a father whose son was shot and killed while driving his car in Detroit on his birthday. I remember him describing how, for months afterwards, he could not stop himself from driving down that street looking for his son's killers. He too joined a support group. Later he was instrumental in getting Michigan legislation to ban the sale of gangster trading cards that were being sold in the state. Like baseball trading cards, these cards had a picture of a gangster on the front and on the back detailed the murders and crimes committed.

Reaction

Lesson

Lesson: This father demonstrated that, in his efforts to cope with his son's murder, he needed to do something. "I just can't sit around and do nothing," he told me. At first that need was driven by the primitive survival response of his nervous system. It was not rational and defied logic. He did not even know who the killer was at the time. What he was doing brought some momentary relief, but also put him in some danger. Only after he started attending the POMC support group was his primal nervous energy directed into accomplishing something meaningful. **When surviving children and adults alike are not provided supportive, self-regulating opportunities to do something meaningful, this *need to do something* can take the form of more primal, sometimes dangerous survivor responses.**

Twenty-Four Hours a Day

I remember a mother's son who was shot and killed on her wedding anniversary, which was also Valentine's Day. I remember her describing how, one year later, she was still looking at that spot where he was killed in front of their house. I remember her describing how, when she was holding a picture of her son, she talked to him, but, "he never answers back." I remember her describing how she would be cooking something on the stove and would walk away forgetting that the burner was still on. And, I remember her describing how, if she would have let him buy her an anniversary gift when he asked, he wouldn't have been where he was shot. He would be alive today. I remember her telling me that her surviving son was rarely at home anymore, her older daughter no longer came over to visit and that her husband no longer talked to anyone in the family.

Reaction

Lesson

Lesson: This mother's response embodies much of what has been described in previous experiences when both children and adults alike became vulnerable because trauma-informed intervention was not provided. This mother cannot avoid the constant physical reminders, which keep her lost in that traumatic experience, as if it just happened yesterday. This is also the reason why avoiding physical reminders can be helpful and necessary for some. She blames herself for her son's death because of what she did just prior to his murder. She shares the same guilt experienced by others in the midst of trauma related to what they did or did not do at the time. She also describes the loss of concentration and short-term memory seen in so many trauma victims, including students who go without immediate trauma-specific support. The siblings no longer want to be at home because of reminders, but primarily because of their mother's ongoing reactions. Younger siblings, as described earlier, who do not have the option of avoiding the traumatized parent, bring their worry, fear, anger and sense of abandonment with them into the classroom. All of these factors lead this mother to consider suicide. Children, who feel emotionally abandoned by their parents, travel the same path. They see no end to all that is happening to them and around them.

Only after this mother sought help from Parents of Murdered Children (the same support group the adults in the previous stories attended) did her life begin to change. The support that she received no longer left her feeling alone. Hope was established as she realized that others in the group were not only finding ways to cope, but also developing a new purpose in their lives. **This was not a therapy group. It was a support group offering the same kind of beneficial support a trauma-informed school response can provide to students and staff in crisis. This helps prevent and minimize the kind of problems that can develop when that support is not immediately provided.**

In Chapters Three, Four, Five and Six, educators and responders exposed to 9/11, Sandy Hook Elementary, Virginia Tech, and Chardon, Ohio, tell their stories and the valuable lessons they learned. However, before detailing their experiences I present the brief experiences I had dealing with survivors of the Gulf War, today's military families and the impact multiple deployments have on the children and the parent who stays behind. The number of students of military families in our schools today, the prevalence of PTSD experienced by those parents returning from service, its impact on the family and the effects of multiple deployment on children warrant the attention of those who work with or spend time with children from military families.

Multiple Deployments: The Worries of Children of Military Families

Children can be exposed to war and violence directly and indirectly. Often the children indirectly exposed are thought to be doing fine because they were not in the war arena itself. **The children of military families must also be considered potential victims of war, even when away from the war zone.** Research documents children of military families have more emotional difficulties than those from nonmilitary families when compared with national samples (Chandra et al., 2009). In a new and a more recent study, military deployments are now tied to teen depression (Raven, 2013).

Several years ago, a colleague and I had the opportunity to spend time with children whose parent or parents had been deployed multiple times. We were not introduced as psychologists, but as people who were simply there to spend time with them while their parents attended a number of lectures.

Understanding that children have numerous worries, I was curious to see whether the worries of military children might be different. Understanding the power of drawing, when used in a structured format, the children were given illustrated worksheets related to worry that were developmentally appropriate. They were asked to write down their worries within the graphic illustration presented on the worksheet. The younger children were also asked to color the animal that showed how big or small their worry was for them. The adolescents were asked to rate their worries on a scale of 1 to 5, with 5 being as "big as it gets." They were asked to write that rating next to their worry.

We had no previous contact with these children. We spent an hour with the younger children, 90 minutes with the older groups. This first activity took about two-thirds of the time available with each group. The children were engaged in a fun activity that allowed them to be creative with construction paper, glue, feathers, pipe cleaners, crayons, colored pencils and paints. The worry activity followed this fun activity and was met with the same enthusiasm as the initial expressive activity.

The question presented to all children was to identify one of their worries. It could be about anything, not necessarily about their families. The following worries were those from the 6- to 9-year-old group.

- My dad has to leave to deploy
- My dad will leave again
- That my mother other will not get better from her sickness and that I might get kidnapped or hurt
- I will get shot
- My family
- Making new friends when I move again
- Getting picked up on time
- When I get bullied around
- Someone breaking into the house
- My mom will go away
- Feels gray at grandma's house not so happy

Sixteen of these children rated their worry from moderate to severe. Six children identified the worry as small.

Following are the worries of the 10- to 13-year-old group:

- When my dad goes away because of his job and not coming back
- My sister getting hurt or lost

- Making my parents happy every moment of the day
- If my dad doesn't come home
- My mom not being safe
- My mom and dad not coming back home
- Mostly about my mom and dad as they are getting a divorce and it is pretty frustrating to me and my sisters
- What's going to happen to me at school
- Even when my dad calls home, I worry if he is okay
- Grades in school
- Myself, school and family

The teenage group (13–18 years) was also informed that the worry could be any event in their lives, not necessarily worry about their family. Their worries were:

- My dad not going to be there
- I won't be able to get through eighth grade
- Passing high school
- My dad moving out-of-state
- That he is not safe
- My grades slipping and disappointing my parents
- That my dad won't come home
- About not doing good in school and sports
- My parents fighting over divorcing

This group was also asked what they thought nonmilitary teens should know about them. Their responses included:

- Life isn't always happy
- A lot of changes are made
- They (nonmilitary children) are lucky because they get to spend a lot of time with their parents while ours are gone for six months
- That we have more responsibilities than most people
- Knowing your mom and dad might die tomorrow
- That we have to move a lot and it's difficult

The worries do seem age appropriate with the teens worrying about doing well in school. In each case, there is the worry of a parent not returning, a number of safety and security worries, as well as uncertainties related to the family. The majority of children and teens rated their worries from moderate to severe. If we had more time to explore their worries, I am sure they would also worry about their deployed parent returning physically and emotionally well and all the changes in the home routines, roles and responsibilities when that parent does return.

When we met with these children, there was still little reported about the impact of deployment on children in military families. Today PTSD, depression and the well-being of the "stay-at-home" parent are critical issues being documented. Perhaps, with this new awareness and prevalence of depression and anxiety, military families will receive more trauma-specific assistance.

Reaction

Lesson

Lesson: **What we learned was this one nonintrusive drawing activity brought us quickly and safely into the private world of these children in ways that simply would not be accomplished by the more intrusive approach of verbally questioning them about their worries. We learned that such insight is obtained quickly when using a medium children feel safe using.**

The Gulf War

My experience with survivors of the Gulf War demonstrated the universal ways children depict their memories, how those memories are not hindered by issues of diversity and how a great deal can be accomplished to help survivors with their reactions. This is especially true when that intervention is structured and provides a vehicle for communicating what is limited by language. That experience led to the development of the school-based, psychoeducational, evidence-based programs titled, *I Feel Better Now* (Steele, Kuban, Lemerand, & Ginns-Gruenberg, 2000) and *Structured Sensory Interventions for Traumatized At-Risk and Adjudicated Adolescents* (Steele & Jacobs, 2007).

Near the end of the Gulf War in 1992, a colleague and I were invited by the Kuwaiti government to train members of that community to assist the survivors of that war and its citizens. Many struggled with a number of mental health issues and were experiencing PTSD. There was no formal mental health system in Kuwait at that time, so help was limited. Although we spent the majority of our time working with adults, we did have the opportunity to spend time with a number of children exposed to the atrocities of the Gulf War. Their spirit and excitement while with us was truly amazing. At the end of the day, they presented us with a number of drawings depicting their experiences of that war. Years later, following the attack on the United States on 9/11, the children directly exposed to that situation also provided us with a number of drawings. When comparing the drawings they have many similarities.

Reaction

Lesson

Lesson: Drawing becomes a vehicle for communicating across diverse populations and transcends the limits of language. It allows children to use symbols accepted in their culture to depict the universal subjective experiences of trauma, in this case war—the terror, hurt and anger, revenge, accountability, feeling unsafe and powerless. In many cases the images used to depict their experiences are very similar regardless of cultural differences. Researchers document that children reveal much more about their experiences after drawing than when simply questioned about what happened. It makes sense for drawing to be an integral part of recovery interventions. The benefits of drawing as an intervention are well documented by research (Steele & Kuban, 2013).

Adult Survivors of the Gulf War

Our primary purpose in Kuwait was to provide intervention practices and skills to the adults in the groups we were meeting with in order to assist them in their efforts to help surviving victims. Near the end of our second week with our initial group, one of the women volunteered to take part in the intervention process I was developing. This is now a core evidence-based trauma intervention for children and adults (Steele & Kuban, 2013). The purpose was to demonstrate some of the strategies we had been teaching. At the time she volunteered, I had no idea that she had been traumatized by what happened to her husband. It was interesting that, in the days prior to the intervention, she always had with her a very thick book with a bright red cover that I refer to as the *Book of Martyrs (unpublished)*. It was a very gruesome book, as it basically presented photographs of all the tortured victims in their tortured state. It was the country's way of giving some meaning to those who lost their lives to save their country and one another, yet it was not a book most would spend time looking at given the grotesque pictures of tortured children and adults. I discovered she was struggling with a number of PTSD reactions at the very beginning of the session. Her husband was abruptly taken from her, tortured and died in that war.

Before beginning, I stressed how important it was for her to feel free to say "yes" or "no" to anything that was asked of her. I also stressed that she could end the intervention any time she wished. Her safety was a priority. Her first drawing was a picture of her husband's tortured face. His eyes were drawn shut. She later indicated they were missing. She was able to convey a number of details related to the torture of her husband. In fact, if you saw her initial drawing you would be able to identify her husband in the *Book of Martyrs*. Although she completed a number of drawings, she was unable to draw a picture of her husband's face with his eyes open so we might see what he looked like before all this happened. She was asked to do this initially, in hopes of reconnecting her to a living memory of him, rather than remain stuck on the tortured memory of his face.

The intervention consisted of one evening session and the final session the following morning. In the evening session, she completed several of the drawing activities, but also chose not to draw certain aspects, such as her husband's face the way he looked prior to this happening. At the end of the evening session, I carefully prepared her for the remainder of the evening once she arrived home. I wanted her to know when those in her home went to bed and the silence in the house grew louder, she might begin to have additional memories and reactions. I stressed that this would be quite normal and would offer her additional opportunity to make sense of all that happened then and up to this point of time in her life. The next morning before we started the intervention, she walked up to me and presented me with the *Book of Martyrs* saying, "Thank you so much for helping me. I want you to have this to remember how much you have helped all of us." The way she presented herself in that brief moment was not the same person I was providing intervention to the previous evening.

When we began the final session, she talked about how she began remembering more in the quiet evening hours at home. At one point she indicated she started calling people from her memories to verify that what she was remembering was what actually took place the way she remembered. She shared that information with us because some of it was also about her husband when he was alive; I asked her once again if she could now draw us a picture of her husband alive and what he looked like before all this happened. She was now able to draw a picture of her husband's face with his eyes opened, the way he looked before he was tragically taken from her.

Once completed, I gave her permission to sit quietly and to take as much time as needed to say all of the things she would have liked to have said to him before he was taken from her. She sat quietly for a few moments and then turned to us and said, "I need to talk to him out loud." In essence, she made us a living witness to the love that they shared. It was a very special and very moving moment for all of us; certainly one I will never forget. It taught me several valuable lessons. Overnight, she had disconnected herself from that tortured memory. In this morning session, she literally handed that memory over to me when she gave me the *Book of Martyrs*. Many of her PTSD reactions diminished in the weeks that followed. She made a special visit to see us several months later when we had returned to spend time with another group. She said her life was so much better since that brief time spent on that one intervention.

Reaction

```
┌─────────────────────────────────────────────────────────┐
│                                                           │
│   Lesson                                                  │
│                                                           │
│                                                           │
│                                                           │
│                                                           │
│                                                           │
└─────────────────────────────────────────────────────────┘
```

Lesson: It was this one experience that convinced me to develop a more comprehensive intervention using drawing as the primary medium for addressing the universal subjective experiences of trauma. It taught me how many valuable lessons can be learned from survivors when we give them the opportunity to tell their story in their own way through the use of drawing.

Summary

Lesson: The major lesson these experiences teach us is that ultimately no community is immune from terribly traumatic incidents. There is absolutely no reason not to be prepared.

This brings us to the stories of the educators who were directly involved in caring for the survivors of 9/11, Sandy Hook Elementary, Virginia Tech and Chardon, Ohio. Each presents valuable lessons about caring for survivors and the larger school community. The lessons contain additional critical recovery strategies recommended also be included in the recovery intervention process. They certainly can help schools and community responders become far better prepared for similar incidents. Even the death of one student or one staff person and the survivors left behind requires the use of some of these strategies and the lessons they teach about recovery.

Survivors and Responders 2
of September 11, 2001:
What You Did Not
Read About

"There was no public transportation. We couldn't get out. Parents couldn't get to us. Communication was impossible."

"Day had turned to night and the children were led uptown through ash and smoke. People passing were covered in dust and bleeding. Many teachers walked backwards for blocks with their students maintaining eye contact with them, exhorting them to 'Look at me' so the children wouldn't see the horror around."

"It took one mother over two hours to walk to get to our school, only to find we had put her child on the bus, which we couldn't be sure had gotten through."

"We knew there was death all around, yet 'no one had died,' everyone was missing. We didn't know what to say."

"There was no access to Superintendents. Decisions that previously could only be made by Superintendents—we now had to make."

"The only way I could get to my school was to park my car miles away and walk."

"Assault rifles, soldiers and cement walls were surrounding our area. At one point, children being playful and curious jumped or crawled over the cement barricades, only to be met by the barrels of rifles."

These comments capture just a few of the experiences New York school staff faced that horrible day. I consulted with many first responders in the days following 9/11 and trained a number of professionals throughout the following year. However, it was not until I spent the day with staff from the New York City school system that the scope of all that needs attending to in such situations was revealed. The media rarely wrote about the impact this act of terror had on the schools in the area. Even the largest research project ever conducted on children's reactions to critical situations failed to interview teachers. Their stories were quite revealing.

One principal (from Lower Manhattan), who was known as a good military-style principal said, "I always knew I was responsible for my students. I never knew I was responsible for their lives."

This statement reflects the tremendous responsibility of principals and all school staff, especially in today's world when catastrophic events and violence takes the lives of so many. This was the case at Sandy Hook Elementary and the case on 9/11. At Sandy Hook Elementary, student and staff were in direct danger of being killed. The lives of students and staff in Lower Manhattan on 9/11 were not directly in danger, yet the lessons they learned apply to all potentially dangerous and deadly situations.

Pierre Lehmuller, executive director of the New York Elementary School Principals Association, Grace Julian, principal of Murry Bergtraum High School, Sheila Brown, Community Schools guidance counselor, and Marjorie Robbins, director of Pupil Personnel Services, who were in these positions at the time, each had unique experiences they shared one year following 9/11. For ease of reading, many of their responses are paraphrased. In some cases what is said is the lesson itself; that lesson will be in bold. In other cases we ask for your reactions and the lessons you derive from their experiences and, as in Chapter One, that experience will be followed with the possible lesson(s) that each experience teaches us.

An Administrator's Initial Reaction

Pierre gave a view that I never read about in all the reported accounts of that day. "What many do not realize," he said, "is the attack and collapse of the Twin Towers was clearly visible to the majority of school staff and students in New York. Contrary to popular belief, schools in the area were on a higher elevation than the financial district. Thousands of children, from 13 schools, were direct witnesses to the collapse of the Towers, to people jumping to their deaths and to that dark cloud of ash. Thousands of students' families also lived in that area. Battery Park, for example, has numerous condos and apartments that housed the families of the students who attended the nearby schools. When the Towers collapsed, those students' families and thousands of others in the area were locked in total darkness by that cloud of ash that covered miles." As Pierre tells us, one year later, he still recalls this memory as if it were yesterday.

<table>
<tr><td>

Reaction

</td></tr>
</table>

<table>
<tr><td>

Lesson

</td></tr>
</table>

Lesson: When trauma occurs, witnesses, even those who are not in harm's way, may need as much support as those directly victimized. We can imagine the panic and terror everyone experienced at that moment in time. There were thousands of students who were never in physical danger; yet what they witnessed and experienced that day changed their lives forever. Thousands of children in the Lower Manhattan and surrounding area were assigned the diagnosis of PTSD.

A Principal's Account

Grace reported that Lower Manhattan became a war zone totally locked down by police. No one knew if there was going to be more attacks to come. The transit system was shut down as well as the expressways. One Police Plaza was right next to Grace's school. The Murry Bergtraum School of Business was a few blocks from the Twin Towers. The presence of cement barricades, large sand trucks surrounding Police Plaza and the police armed with AK-47s remained for weeks.

Lower Manhattan was off-limits to all except for those who worked there or were students. The only way in was to have the proper identification. Even Grace was not allowed to cross the barriers when she appeared one day without identification. When she was able to contact the commander, whom she knew well, he told her that many of the police protecting the area were from other precincts and did not know the regulars. And as Grace said, "They didn't care who I said I was, they were not going to let anyone in without the proper identification. It took us a considerable amount of time to get ID badges made for all the school staff and students. You can imagine the problems we had with students' forgetting them. It was frustrating and annoying, even though it was for our safety. And kids being kids, they did things at times that terrified us. One day a few of our students decided to climb over the barricades around Police Plaza. We were terrified that one of the police might act too quickly."

Reaction

Lesson

Lesson: Crisis teams must always be prepared for a new crisis developing as a result of the turmoil and the efforts to control that turmoil. What is acceptable and not acceptable behavior must be clearly communicated. Administrators must be ready to respond.

Since incidents like Columbine and 9/11, school safety plans have a chain of command, which generally involves at least three individuals from different agencies as well as law enforcement. Most schools have met with their city, county and state officials to detail roles and responsibilities in potentially deadly situations.

During 9/11, securing Lower Manhattan was needed. However, what people were not prepared for were their reactions to the "military-like compound" that was created—the presence of force, the visible assault rifles, and the problems created by having to move through checkpoints every day. A crisis can create new challenges, which may lead to other crises. That was the case many years ago, when I was assisting schools that were dealing with student suicides. The reactions of one group of students following the suicide of their peer created another crisis for the school.

In this case, the student's name was Ryan. He was a popular kid. One night his father found him hanging in the garage. He was in a coma for a week before he died. As could be expected, Ryan's friends were in an emotional crisis. Others exhibited behaviors that were not expected. Some adolescents (true to form) handled the event with the callousness that some youth can show. "They were heard chanting in the hallways 'R-Y-A-N. If he comes back, we'll hang him again!'" The ensuing fights resulted in suspensions and added even more tension to the already overcharged atmosphere. Students' lives were not in danger immediately following the suicide of their friend; however, the reaction of some to what happened changed that for a number of students.

What to Do

Grace said that when the Towers were hit, the police were told initially to evacuate their building because they thought they might be the next target. Because Murry Bergtraum School of Business was right next to Police Plaza, the police immediately told the school to also evacuate. At that time in New York, no principal had the authority to call for an evacuation without obtaining approval from the superintendent. All those related protocols changed that day as decisions had to be made quickly.

Reaction

Lesson

Lesson: When those in a leadership role are not prepared to make major decisions during a crisis, it creates additional anxiety for them and can place those in crisis at greater risk. Today's safety plans are far more specific about the decisions needed by administrators, yet I have met many administrators who have not looked at those crisis plans. That underlying attitude *that it won't happen here* is insidious, as Sandy Hook Elementary discovered. In a time of crisis, we do not want to use valuable time to figure out what it is we need to be doing. We need to respond immediately with very specific tasks being initiated simultaneously.

Controlling the Situation

Murry Bergtraum School had a student enrollment of close to 3,000 students. There were 10 assistant principals at the time. Not all students were in school the first hour of 9/11, some were in the area on their way to school that day. The school also has several floors. Windows looked out toward the Towers. When the first Tower was hit, the students in the building saw what happened and had many questions. When Grace found out, she went on the PA system and told them that a plane hit the tower. She urged them to stay calm, promising to keep them informed as soon as she had more information.

At about the time the second tower was hit, the class change bell rang and all the students left their classrooms. Now they were even more frightened because they were hearing many different accounts from their peers about what they were witnessing; Grace knew she needed to get them back in their classes quickly and keep them there. She turned off the bell system and then went to use the PA system to try to redirect their attention and get them back in the classroom. "I'm the principal," she said, "I knew they would listen." Unfortunately the PA system stopped working. She had no bullhorn. Even though there were 10 assistant principals, getting them back into their classrooms was not easy.

Reaction

Lesson

Lesson: Access to *backup* **not only applies to staff, but to communication systems**. Students were direct witnesses to what was happening. This meant maintaining control was even more essential to prevent behaviors that would put others at risk. It was also essential to initiating behaviors that would keep all as safe as possible. The loss of immediate communication with all students magnified the risk. Grace had great leadership qualities and had fostered that in her staff. The fact that police were in the building almost immediately prevented things from getting worse. Grace said that their presence, more than anything, made the difference at that point. Grace's decisive leadership style was also critical.

Staying Behind

When they were told to evacuate, they were told that they could only go north, even though many of the children's normal routes were in opposite directions. This obviously intensified their fears. In addition, there were 25 severely physically challenged students. Many staff evacuated with their students while several stayed behind with the physically challenged children. Several of the children were in wheelchairs. Grace said that one of her staff wheeled one of these children the entire evacuation route, which was a few miles.

Buses were needed to evacuate the others, but cell phones were not available to them at the time. Fortunately, one of her staff was a friend of the owner of a check-cashing business across from the school. He let Grace and his friend use his phone to arrange for the buses. This took a considerable amount of time because of the chaos. The buses could not get access to the school until 8:00 that night. Staff stayed with those students until all were safely on the buses. You can image the parents' fears during this time when it was difficult to contact them or for them to get into the area.

Reaction

Lesson

Lesson: Identify beforehand those staff willing to stay behind if neces-sary to assist students with special needs. Also in a time of crisis, prior relationships do matter. Crisis teams ought to involve neighboring business owners in a meeting or two to discuss ways they might be of help when a crisis impacts their community.

Parents

Because so many parents work in the area, they rushed to the schools want-ing their children immediately. Common sense told Grace she needed to slow the parents down and attempt to reunite them with their children in an orderly fashion. With the help of staff and, fortunately, the police, the pro-cess was fairly orderly. However, what she was not prepared for were parents wanting to take several of the children with them because they lived in the same building or on the same block. There was no protocol for this. It came at a time when there was still a great deal of fear that something else might happen. Taking into account the safety of the children, Grace took detailed information from parents allowing those asking to take other students to do so. It was a difficult decision.

Reaction

Lesson

Lesson: Plan ahead for those crises when the physical safety of stu-dents is threatened and parents are asking to take their child and their child's friends with them. Determine the information you need to record and how the parents of those other children will be contacted.

Where Are You Going?

Sheila reported that in one of the schools a father picked up his 9-year-old child. They were signed out using the proper release forms. An hour later the mother came to get her child. Remember, cell phones weren't working, transit systems were shut down and barricades prevented people from using their normal routes home. When the mother asked where her husband took her son, no one had an answer.

Reaction

Lesson

Lesson: We learned that we needed to add a column to the parent's release form that indicated where that parent was planning to take their child.

Overly Activated Parents

Grace also reported that many parents understandably arrived at her school hysterical. "We had to decide," she said, "whether it was best to release their child to those parents." She decided to move those parents to a different area away from the students until her staff could calm them down and be sure that they knew the best available route to get home before releasing those students to those parents. "We were lucky," she said, "because we knew that several on my staff had good experience responding to parents who are agitated and out of control."

Reaction

Lesson

Lesson: **Several staff on every crisis team need to have good experience and comfort levels when working with upset adults (staff included) when the building is in crisis.** When parents are in crisis because they fear for their child, their decisions and behaviors can place both at risk. Knowingly releasing a child to an upset parent can have significant legal and emotional ramifications for all involved should something happen. **It is recommended when dealing with agitated adults, especially those whom you do not know, that a male and female crisis team member meet with that adult to help them de-escalate. In addition, it is better for two team members to agree on the best action in a crisis than for one person to carry all that responsibility alone.** Being a crisis responder is filled with stress because of the exposure to so many reactions and unknowns. It is also highly stressful because of the many quick decisions that need to be made, often with little information. When two people make those decisions together, that stress is minimized and a check and balance approach supported.

Prior Relationships Matter

Marjorie said, "You can never have enough parent meetings. When it came time to reopen schools, it wasn't just a matter of physical readiness but community readiness. Some communities were still worried about the safety of their children. The school system and the Mayor's office wanted to say everything was returning to normal, that kids were back in school, but some communities were not ready to be pushed. Keeping in mind that there were numerous bomb threats and ongoing evacuations, parents needed to feel a sense of control."

Reaction

Lesson

Lesson: "We learned that involving parents in the decision to reopen a school was essential to their feeling safer about letting their children go back to that school. We found the schools that had greater parent involvement before 9/11 were able to reopen sooner than those who had less parent involvement before the events of 9/11. The majority of students returned to the schools where parents were more involved."

When Verbal Reassurance Fails

Marjorie also reported that many parents worried about putting their children on school buses when schools reopened. All the precautions that were now in place were explained, but that was not enough for parents. Staff rode with their students on the buses until parents and the children felt safer.

Lesson: Engaging in behaviors that demonstrate support for parent concerns is far more powerful and beneficial than trying to use reason and verbal reassurance.

Staff Flexibility

Grace decided to reopen Murry Bergtraum School on September 13. They developed a lesson plan to present to teachers on how to talk to their students about what happened. When it was presented to the staff, a number of them said they couldn't follow those recommendations. They just wanted to teach their subject. School counselors were provided in those classrooms to spend time normalizing the many reactions they knew students were likely having and answering their questions before those teachers began to teach.

Reaction

Lesson

Lesson: Just as children in crisis need choices, adults need choices as well to feel safe and be able to best manage while in crisis.

Crisis Intervention Not Always a Priority

Pierre indicated that some schools reopened on September 13, some on September 18, and some remained closed for months. Students from the closed schools were taken in by other schools. The class schedule was changed to 7am to noon and from 1pm to 6pm. This created numerous issues similar to what Houston schools experienced following Hurricane Katrina. There were cultural conflicts, lack of resources and space issues. There were no extracurricular activities and no access to student records. There were also numerous transportation issues. Many staff, especially administrators, were not ready to participate in crisis intervention because their major concerns were about the resources students and teachers needed. In some classrooms there was a severe shortage of desks. Gymnasiums were used in some situations, which as can be imagined presented a number of challenges.

Reaction

```
┌─────────────────────────────────────────────────────────────┐
│                                                               │
│   Lesson                                                      │
│                                                               │
│                                                               │
│                                                               │
│                                                               │
│                                                               │
│                                                               │
└─────────────────────────────────────────────────────────────┘
```

Lesson: This is a story that is likely to be repeated many times over in the coming years. Being prepared ahead of time is the easy part. The hard part is not to hold on to the false belief that such a situation will never happen. This belief erodes preparedness and places all at greater risk.

Weeks, Months Later It Is Still a Part of Us

Marjorie told several stories about the challenges her staff presented because of the ongoing fear of something else happening. A couple weeks after the attack, a group of staff was meeting on the seventh floor of a large building. When a business across the street was ordered to evacuate because of a possible bomb, the school office building was not ordered to do the same. The staff response was, "We're out of here." They left. The fear of being trapped on higher floors was difficult to overcome. They decided to relocate staff to the second floor of a smaller building and brought in resources to debrief them because they were in no way ready to resume their duties.

However, even when routines had been established, staff were still easily agitated. "One principal smashed in a door during a fire drill practice because he couldn't find his key to open it."

Sheila told the story of a powdery substance being found in a classroom by a teacher about a month after schools had reopened. The teacher immediately contacted the office while removing her students from the classroom. The school was immediately put on lockdown. The Hazmat team arrived quickly and started to check for anthrax. What they discovered was that it was the sugary content from a student's candy straw. The straw was found on the floor. The teacher who found the substance didn't stop to ask the student what it was, but just immediately went into survival mode. The front office did the same. Prior to 9/11 the responses would have been much different.

Reaction

Lesson

Lesson: Having help readily available for staff far beyond the initial crisis period of four to six weeks must be part of the planned crisis response. Be prepared for a variety of reactions in the aftermath of a crisis. People will not respond as they have previously. Depending on the terror or fear that a crisis can induce, the level of exposure, the loss of life and the many environmental factors introduced, survival reactions can linger for some time. We also learned that for some, any action or element similar to what happened on 9/11 triggered primal survival behaviors.

Staff and Family Turnover

In later months many families and staff left the area because the air quality was causing severe respiratory problems for so many. They also left because the close proximity and constant reminders were too emotionally overpowering.

Reaction

Lesson

Lesson: **Be prepared for staff turnover following a major crisis. It happened in New York and it happened in Connecticut following the terror at Sandy Hook Elementary. Also seasoned substitutes will generally function best in the aftermath of a crisis. However, all substitutes on a school's roster should be provided the same training as staff related to responsibilities during a crisis and the possible reactions experienced by students as well as themselves.**

When a Parent Is Missing and Likely Dead

When schools were scheduled to reopen, they didn't know which students might have a parent who worked in the towers or were police officers or firefighters. They scrambled and found as many student cards as they could and tried to identify the parent's workplace by using zip codes. In a number of cases, they were able to identify those students who may have suffered the loss of their parent. **Lesson: This provided some help in determining the number of resources that might be needed to help those students. Having a backup records system is critical.**

Making the Call

They did not know why some students did not return. Was it due to transportation issues, because they or their parents were not ready for them to return or because their parent(s) had died? Making the call to see what had happened was very difficult. Marjorie indicated they needed help and guidance with this.

Sheila said that because many parents never returned home that day, it made it more difficult to talk with the kids about the loss of their parent. Many were not confirmed dead for several days while rescue teams continued searching through the rubble for survivors. These efforts continued beyond September 13 when some schools reopened.

Reaction

Lesson

Lesson: In this case, counselors were dealing with aspects of those miss-ing in action and issues of anticipatory grief. There are many resources (see Appendix) that can help shape how children are approached under these conditions. This resource should be part of a crisis manual. Despite how a parent may suddenly die—or for that matter a student—that child and those student's peers expect the adults left in their lives (teachers/counselors) to say something. What is conveyed will differ based upon the cause of death, such as suicide versus homicide. It is important to know the many alternative ways to discuss possible death and death itself and to have these available as scripts in the crisis plan. In some cases, especially with younger children, reading a book related to the loss of a parent/sibling/peer can be more helpful than anything we might have to say at the time.

When Talk Fails

Grace reported that as she walked through the school, there were a number of times she asked students how they were doing. She reported that, "Many just said they didn't want to talk about what happened; they just wanted to do their schoolwork. However, others were visibly struggling." What is sel-dom mentioned in the stories about that day are the number of people who jumped from the Towers to their death and the many kids who saw this. This and so many other physical aspects of what they witnessed and experienced understandably left many struggling. Marjorie found at times with those who were struggling that talking to them was of very little value. "They did their best," she said, " when drawing or engaged in a variety of different kinds of art activities and other expressive activities like music."

Lesson: When children are in a state of terror they are operating primarily from their midbrain, where reason and logic do not exist. When operating primarily from the midbrain/survival brain much of what is said cannot be heard or comprehended. Therefore, it is critical to meet children where they are living at the time by engaging them in a variety of activities that are safe and allow them to express themselves in ways in which they may not have the words or language to do so.

A First-Person Account

Sheila, the guidance counselor, gave a first-person account of her initial reactions. "I saw what was happening on television when the first Tower was hit and then the second Tower. I left my office to go to the downtown area not really understanding the magnitude of all that happened. To give a sense of how I was impacted by what I saw on television and how I was processing it all, I went outside and was searching for a taxi before I realized there was no traffic so I started to walk. As I walked, others layered in ash, were rushing past me uptown. I saw groups of people huddled around cars listening to the radio. I knew this couldn't be good but still it hadn't totally hit me. When I got to our receiving hospital, where the injured would be immediately taken in, doctors in their white coats were standing by a row of gurneys. The gurneys were empty. No one was being brought to the emergency room. I didn't know what to think other than things were not good.

"When I got to the school, which was near the hospital, I had yet another reaction. There were some parents leaving with their children. Bottled water and snacks were piled in the hall. I had no idea where they came from. This was the school that was receiving students from the downtown schools. When I walked in no one was crying, it seemed calm, kids were playing board games and otherwise seemed to be entertained by staff. When I was told that hundreds had likely died, I realized nothing was fine. Many of the students and staff had parents and loved ones who worked in the Towers or were police officers or firemen who I now realized were likely killed. This is when I realized everyone was in shock including myself.

"I knew one of the teachers whose husband worked in the Towers. I told her I would take over for her so she could leave to find her husband not fully understanding that this would likely never happen because of all the chaos, even if he were alive. Many didn't know who died until later that night when they didn't return to their loved ones. She said 'no' that she would stay with her students until parents arrived and the students left with them. To me this was remarkable. I also remember a mother who had an older child in the school. She was in the downtown area with her 5-year-old daughter and had just walked backwards from that area to the school, shielding her daughter from the chaos, the panic and the ash. They gave me strength to do whatever I could do."

Sheila's account demonstrates that the generosity and resilience of those in crisis can inspire us. However, she added the following comment, "I didn't have our crisis plan with me. I certainly couldn't remember what our plan may have suggested for some of what was happening. At that point, I can only tell you I did what I did. I do remember we all needed help."

Lesson: Even for professionals, the reality of what has happened may take time to actively become real. The initial shock to our nervous systems can make first impressions and reactions misleading. If we do not have some direction, some sense of what we need to do, when the reality that "Nothing is fine" sets in, all we can do is what we do. What we do may or may not help.

Without a well-structured crisis plan available as a quick resource for getting us back into our thinking brain and giving us very specific actions to initiate, what we do not do may also be very critical to the immediate and long-term well-being of everyone involved.

Resource Materials

Marjorie indicated they received a great deal of help from the staff at the New York Child Study Program. They brought them resource materials to give parents, normalized a lot of their reactions and the students' reactions, talked about PTSD and made suggestions as to how they could approach the students.

Lesson: These are materials and guidelines that need to be in every crisis plan but are of little value if they are not immediately accessible.

Outside Help

Marjorie also said that schools needed to be protected from the onslaught of those who want to help in a crisis. "The last thing staff or students wanted to have to worry about," she said, "were strangers."

Lesson: Collaborate. Know those professionals you might need to call for help before you are in a situation where you need them.

Ethnicity Issues

In the introduction, Pierre mentioned the ethnic issues that emerged. Some students had to be protected and supported. An Arabic family, who owned the store a block away from the school their children attended, refused to send their children to school when it reopened. They feared for their safety. When the principal discovered this, he took some of his staff to the store and had them buy groceries. He then said to those parents, "Please send your children back to school, it will be okay."

Reaction

Lesson

Lesson: Ethnic issues aside, reaching out to those school families who may still be very frightened for the safety of their children, no matter the cause or reason, needs to be part of the crisis plan. When a principal— who carries tremendous authority—does this, it is as if he/she is speaking for the entire school. It means a great deal to parents.

Things We Learned

I asked if each of my guests could summarize the lessons they learned or were still learning. Following are their responses. We learned that:

- **We needed to be like pregnant women who have their bags packed.** Schools need to have ready-to-go packets with student lists, parent releases, water, snacks, etc.
- **When you think it's over it's not.** "The one-year anniversary was just a few weeks ago. Children were in school for four days before September 11.

The news media was stirring things up with all its rebroadcasts of the news that day. We needed to spend time with both staff and students to normalize all their reactions and be available for those who found the anniversary more difficult to manage."

- **Schools need to be self-sufficient when it comes to a crisis.** They need trained staff with assigned roles because the reality is help may not be available for some time.
- **If you are going to use identification badges, list on the back the critical protocol for staff to follow in an emergency.**
- **We needed a buddy, to not be alone during a crisis and in the days that followed.**
- **Prior relationships with our neighbors and businesses in our area do matter.** Many of them left their businesses to help us with the students. They brought water, let us use their phones and just became another adult presence that helped children feel safer.
- **Safety plans need to have alternatives, especially around evacuation.**
- **Competing agencies have** *egos.* Those we found provided the most appropriate help were the ones we had prior relationships with and who understood our needs as well as their limitations.
- **People who sleep on couches get grouchy.** In other words, we learned that we needed to do a better job at self-care.
- **The goodness of people around the world is amazing.** However, we learned we needed to dedicate staff just to talk with and manage all the phone calls, letters and the stuff that was sent to us.
- **When you are stressed, you get really thirsty. Mashed potatoes do help.**
- **A crisis challenges every assumption and detail of what we think we can manage.**
- **At the time of crisis we are forced to do all the things we have (hopefully) talked about and have been trained to do, but never thought we would have to do.**
- **A good leader knows he/she cannot do it alone.**
- **Titles do not matter in a crisis; relationships and colleagues do.**
- **Schools that are about collaboration and have good communication are the ones that can mobilize the quickest.**

Final Question

One of the final questions I asked was about personal reactions these responders and survivors experienced. I wanted to know what one reaction, of all the reactions they had, surprised them the most. Pierre indicated that he can still experience how he was overwhelmed by the massive cloud of ash, knowing that hundreds of thousands of people, their students, were trapped in that total darkness and that many had died. Sheila said she felt like she was swimming underwater, and unable to breathe. She was also surprised at the anger she had for people *uptown* who were going on with life while everyone *downtown* had to go through barricades to get to work and struggle with all the adjustments. Marjorie said she was surprised by how surreal it all felt, that it was like having an out-of-body experience—like being there, but not really there. Grace said that now, whenever she travels, she takes a small kit with her that has a flashlight, bottle of water, a map and a knife. She said, "I was never really afraid of much, which I suppose really helped me as a principal, but now I worry when I have to go someplace."

Two Years After: Pentagon Families

Two years after 9/11, I spent time with family members of those killed at the Pentagon. Everyone was doing better thanks to attending support groups, which also used the program I had developed, *Adults and Parents in Trauma* (Steele & Hayak, 2013), in smaller adjunct groups. They had fewer intrusive recollections and sleepless nights. They found that attending the memorial services the second year was far easier than the first year anniversary. They learned to approach life differently, to focus more on the people in their lives. They learned different ways to regulate the reactions to the many reminders in their environments. They found that some things could not be changed. They found that most people were afraid to talk to them about what happened. They found that people do say hurtful things and not realize it. And, they found that, as they could begin to smile and laugh more frequently, life seemed to be a bit more manageable. Yet, certain responses from the media and the government still angered and retraumatized them for a long time. They were angry at how the attention paid to New Yorkers caused them to feel as if the pain they carried with them was minimized. They talked about how, months later, they were still receiving belongings of their loved ones in the mail, washing away the gains they had made.

Reaction

Lesson

Lesson: Many things can happen that keep the pain and the memories intense. It takes time to move through each day and to gradually discover that the days are getting a bit easier. It takes time to recover and to adjust to the new realities of life. It takes the support of others to help integrate the meaning of such an experience into our new life. If we wish to help our own communities in times of overwhelming loss, we must keep ourselves prepared and informed with best practices. What has been learned in past years still remains critical to our effective response today.

Dr. Elizabeth Haase was one of several volunteers who conducted support groups for the surviving families of those who were killed in the Pentagon. There were six groups: a preschool group, an elementary-school-aged group, an adolescent group, two spouses' groups and a group called others for people who did not fit into the other groups (e.g., siblings, fiancés, parents). The groups began in November of 2001 and ran for three years as a whole. Although the content of these groups will always remain confidential, Elizabeth reflects on what sustained these groups beyond the short-lived efforts of other organizations in the area.

"When we set up the groups for survivors after the Pentagon attack, we were the key groups that lasted in the area. The groups were sponsored under the auspices of the Fairfax-Falls Church Community Services Board of Virginia and organized by Annemarie Bezold. She worked tirelessly and for many long hours in this effort. Without these groups, many of these families would have never received this kind of support. Dr. Steele's intervention program, resources and consultation was of tremendous value and help for us as well as our survivors.

"Our longevity was due to groups forming by word of mouth from survivors who first attended and then reached out to others. It was also because we insisted on keeping the groups private so survivors knew we would not give any information about them to the media. After being overwhelmed by the media onslaught, survivors who came were extremely appreciative of the privacy we provided them.

"We had one group of survivors that was a closed group once it reached 10 people. That group, which I led with a co-facilitator, remained ongoing for over three years and the members continue to be friends and supporters of each other all these years later. They still meet informally and support each other through life's joys and sorrows. Because the group was closed, they were able to really trust and rely on each other. There were a couple of people who left the group because they left the area. We never filled their vacancy with new members. Those who left remained in touch with group members despite their distance. The other group of family members was not as cohesive. I am certain that was because it was not a closed group. Not knowing who would be there from one meeting to the next was just too difficult for some survivors. We also had closed groups for children and teenagers of these families.

"A number of organizations tried to start groups at the time. They failed because they did not wait long enough. **Many of the survivors started coming four or five months after the attacks. They simply couldn't come before because of the life changes they had to manage in those first few months and because they were so traumatized.** After we announced the availability of the groups, we just kept coming every night whether we had participants or not and eventually they came. Before Dr. Steele visited us, all facilitators debriefed together. We listened to all the dreadful stories from the various groups and facilitators. When he met with us, he suggested debriefing together was far too much exposure and that as volunteers we should only process our experiences with our co-facilitator. That greatly enhanced our self-care. My co-facilitator and I realized we were being further traumatized and we began to meet alone. We were greatly helped by that change. We would also check in with each other between the groups. It built a great deal of trust between us and we were able to keep working together with the survivors for a long time.

"There is another very important value to having two facilitators. About eight months before our group ended, my closest friend, who was divorced and had two young children, was dying. My husband and I became one of their main supports. Because I knew I could not do both and I totally trusted my co-facilitator to take over the group, I stopped co-leading the group and she took over. I subbed for her when she could not be there and remained the one person with whom she could debrief when needed. **Despite my leaving, there remained someone they trusted. The continuity my co-facilitator provided was critical and the major reason the formal group continued.** Remember, my leaving was another loss on top of the losses they were already attempting to manage. **Continuity must be planned for when offering trauma victims support.**

"During those groups and while working with survivors from Washington and New York, I got massages at least every two weeks and sometimes weekly. My co-facilitator had a meditation practice for many years and used that throughout her work with our group along with all the other self-care practices we both put in place. We believe that some of the facilitators who did not remain with the groups succumbed to burnout due to poor self-care in the face of witnessing such extreme trauma. I ramped up every self-care technique I had in my arsenal. It was still hard but I was honored to work with these incredible survivors. I tell you this because self-care is just crucial for professionals and staff working with survivors."

Reaction

Lesson

Lesson: Remembering that **healing takes time** will be reinforced again while reading the challenges facing the survivors and responders from Newtown, Connecticut, one year following the Sandy Hook Elementary horror. For those survivors/victims needing help in the months that follow, closed support groups become a safe place, a place where, supported by one another, survivors can simply be themselves, lean on one another and learn together the many different ways to manage their grief, sorrow and traumatic sensations, reactions and memories.

Elizabeth stressed the importance of responder self-care as being essential to providing consistent support to survivors. This too is a message repeated frequently throughout this resource. This book was written to bring you the stories and firsthand accounts of what both survivors and responders found mattered most to them in their efforts to manage in the months that followed their exposure to traumatic events. **Most literature focuses on immediate responses and ignores the challenges both survivors and responders face long after the media attention and outside help has left.** Hopefully the stories and firsthand accounts you have read, and those yet to follow, help you to find and discover what matters most to you as a survivor or responder in your efforts to remain resilient in the months that follow your traumatic experiences and/or exposure to the traumatized survivors you are attempting to support.

Newtown, Connecticut: Dr. Anthony Salvatore— Assistant Principal

3

Dr. Anthony Salvatore—he prefers Tony—was the assistant principal of the middle school in Newtown, Connecticut, and the Safe School Climate Coordinator for the district. He had a very active role in all aspects of the immediate responses and ongoing recovery efforts. He has been with Newtown schools for the past 15 years and had many direct connections with those who died. Dawn Hochsprung, the principal who sacrificed her life for her children, was Tony's mentor and good friend. Of his 139 seventh graders from Sandy Hook, 51 had direct connections with the families whose children and loved ones were killed. As he said, "That's a lot of children to worry about." Had it not been for cutbacks and staff reductions, Tony would have been the assistant principal at Sandy Hook on December 14, 2012.

This becomes significant as he tells his story because of the relationship he had with the principal. "That reel," he said, "plays itself over and over again in my head and with my family as well." When talking with us, two themes continually emerged. The one was *synchronicity,* meaning things happen for a reason. Tony describes a number of experiences he had in the year following the attack to confirm this. He also found in the days, weeks and months that followed he had to say many times, "You've got to be kidding me." He describes some of the unexpected reactions, behaviors and situations that were just unbelievable at the time.

His role as an administrator dictated that he assume a leadership role for the many recovery interventions initiated. As the Safe School Climate Coordinator for the district he was involved with all the staff, the many responders and community families and organizations following the tragedy. Although he describes his experiences as an administrator during this time, he also reveals what so many survivors experienced then and one year later in their efforts to heal. His experiences are presented as he tells them. At times, he will reference Susan; he is speaking of Susan Connelly, his middle school counselor, who spent a good deal of time with survivors and those 51 highly exposed students. She presents the lessons she has learned in Chapter Four. Some of the stories Tony tells reinforce lessons from Chapters One and Two so you are not asked for your reactions. Other stories do ask for your reactions and the lesson they bring to you. And at times very clear lessons emerge as Tony tells his story; these will be in bold.

It's a Marathon

In March, two months after the shooting, Tony called Frank De Angelis of Columbine. He said it was the best thing he could have done at the time, as Frank was extremely helpful. Frank was the principal of Columbine High School when two students killed twelve students and a teacher before killing themselves. He also had been in the line of fire on that fateful day and was somehow spared. Frank was a good person to talk to as he himself had stayed until the school district's kindergarten children of that 1999 tragedy had all graduated high school. One of the things he said to Tony was that **"recovery is a marathon, not a race."** When we think about a marathon we know it takes time to complete. It is critical to pace ourselves and stay within our physical capacity. There are periods that can be exhausting and painful, so much so we want to quit because we believe we cannot make it to the finish. However, we take a drink of water, maybe even walk for a few seconds, catch our breath and start over again going forward. "That has been my experience," Tony said. **"I learned to pace myself by paying attention to my breathing. I learned that when we are under stress we tend to breathe shallow rather than deep."**

It Can't Happen Here

Tony did his dissertation on bullying and bullying intervention, so he had read about the shooting at Columbine and other schools and how often the shooters were victims themselves. In 1993 a good friend of his, George, was superintendent in Wisconsin. On December 2, 1993, George's neighbor, also an assistant principal, was shot by a former 21-year-old student who had a kill list. The assistant principal's name was on that list. At the time, there was very little written about protocol in such situations so George buried himself in reading, studying and developing protocol for emergencies. "What he developed," Tony said, "is much of what FEMA trains us to do now." As Tony's dissertation advisor, George taught Tony the protocols needed in emergencies to help with recovery and the safety of all involved. However getting people to accept the need for such protocols was not very successful.

Tony was responsible for training Newtown staff on lockdowns and safety details. He told us that in his training he always said, "Lockdowns minimize collateral damage." "And invariably," he said, "I would get irate teachers saying that that's a terrible thing to say. That's just horrendous. Why are you saying that? That will never happen in Newtown . . . **Perhaps now,"** he told us, **"people across the country will not fall victim to the false belief that it can't happen to them."**

We Don't Always Know

People expect administrators to know everything but of course this is impossible. Tony said, "Sometimes there are obvious problems we do not recognize as problems because no one has said anything to us." Weeks after this shooting administrators and staff met to share how they were doing. Some of the administrative staff work in the town hall building where they had all the cards that were sent to show support on display. What he did not realize was how this was affecting one of his staff until she shared her experience in the group. She told the group, "This (the cards) just brings it all back every time I have to look at it. It's not that it is not wonderful, but it's like ripping off the scab on a wound. It never heals. I have to look at this almost every day." What makes this story even worse were reports of some staff receiving death threats.

Reaction

Lesson

Lesson: This supports what was mentioned in Chapter One **about creating permanent memorials in schools. It also supports the importance of giving staff a voice, an opportunity to tell their stories. It also demonstrates that violence can precipitate more violence, in this case death threats.** If you recall in Chapter One related to suicide we told the story about those who created an uproar following a suicide attempt of a boy named Ryan whom they did not like—"R-Y-A-N. If he comes back, we'll hang him again." In this violent society we have to be prepared. I was not made aware of this until recently, but an Australian allegedly came up with a video game called "The Slaying at Sandy Hook Elementary School." This video game first has the player shoot the mother, then collect ammo followed by going on a rampage in a school. The alleged developer claims it has a strong anti-gun message. **Violence has a tendency to trigger more violence in many different ways, which needs to be addressed in crisis plans.** This leads us to Tony's next lesson about expect the unexpected or as he stated, "You have got to be kidding."

You Have Got to Be Kidding

Tony told us that the first time the staff got back together after the shooting on Friday was on Sunday. He was there with them because they were his staff and he needed to support them. He added that his staff is one of the "more professional, sensitive, dedicated and feistiest staff he's worked with over the years." The first word to the group was that they needed to talk about timelines. Tony reminded us that these were people who left the building with nothing—no books, no purses, car keys or cars, no cell phones, nothing. All items were impounded for weeks. One staff member stood up and screamed at the top of her lungs, "Are you kidding? That's the first thing you say to us? Not how are we doing or it's good to see you?" Others walked out of the room in tears.

Reaction

Lesson

Lesson: It is essential to everyone's well-being to know how to approach survivors shortly after a traumatic incident. In Chapter One the delayed response of administrators to the killing of a staff person by a student resulted in a great deal of anger and distrust between staff and administration because of administrative failure to immediately communicate with staff. As Tony said about his staff, "If you want them to do something, tell them and they will get it done. But at a time like this, don't call them into a meeting and not spend time seeing how they are doing, what their concerns are at that moment." Understand that administrators are pushed and pulled in many different directions. If you remember, the mayor of New York following 9/11 wanted to report very early that the students were back in school to show the country that they were all doing okay. However, a number of the communities were not ready to go back to school as early as they wanted. **In trauma everyone is a survivor first, a professional second.** If we hope to meet the needs of the organization effectively and efficiently, we must first meet the needs of its survivors.

What Matters Most?

Another "you've got to be kidding me moment" that Tony mentioned was at a meeting that took place before the students returned to school. During that meeting one of the teachers, concerned about liability issues, asked if it would be okay to hug the kids when they came back. The union representative gave the standard reply, "You've got to be careful because . . ." Tony, as the Safe School Climate Coordinator for the district, interrupted and said, "Let's just be very clear on this. I am authorizing hugs to be okay when our kids come in tomorrow." Everyone erupted in applause.

Reaction

```
┌─────────────────────────────────────────────────────────────┐
│                                                               │
│  Lesson                                                       │
│                                                               │
│                                                               │
│                                                               │
│                                                               │
│                                                               │
└─────────────────────────────────────────────────────────────┘
```

Lesson: Litigation is always a concern especially in the midst of a crisis when so much is happening and when reason, logic and common sense are not always at their best. In our efforts to protect children from predators, we have gone to an extreme in our institutions (my opinion). Yes, we need guidelines and consequences when children are mistreated, but **we also need to exercise judgment and common sense and let young children know we are happy to see them and capable of giving them comfort especially when in crisis.**

Insurance

This is yet another "you've got to be kidding me" moment. As President of the Administrators Union, Tony followed up on a union-issued life insurance policy. During his inquiry, it was disclosed that life insurance policies for administrators did not cover homicide. The national union and the insurance agent did fix this. However, the initial disbelief that the family of the principal, who gave up her life for her students, and the families of the other five staff members would not be eligible to receive an insurance payout triggered Tony's "you've got to be kidding me" response. He couldn't help saying, "You really think they wanted to get killed." **Always be prepared for the unexpected.**

Turnover

As has been experienced in the past by school districts that have gone through tragic situations, there was a 70% turnover among administrators and lead teachers who had some administrative duties. Tony indicated that the experts told them that although there was no precedent for this type of tragic event, they have found an average 80% turnover rate of personnel within three to five years following a tragic event.

Reaction

Lesson

Lesson: History does repeat itself. It was experienced in New York following 9/11, in Texas following the 2011 wildfire and in other critical situations. The problem is we often ignore history, which contains many valuable lessons that can help us better prepare. **Unfortunately, the "it can't happen here" belief prevents people from even caring about the lessons that can be learned following any tragic situation.**

A Point of Change

Tony said he was reminded many times that, "We have two ears and only one mouth for a reason—to listen." In a crisis the need to listen to survivors becomes even more important to their healing. He told us that following such a violently catastrophic loss of life that he just began to listen with a different sensitivity to language. "What was interesting for me," he said, "was in the months that followed how sensitive I became to how much violence we use in our language. So I began making a list. One day I presented this list to my staff. I've had more teachers come up and tell me, I hear myself say these things and then talk to myself and try to reframe them.

- "Don't jump the gun." "Give it your best shot!" "What a great shot!"
- "Don't shoot the messenger." "We're dead in the water."
- "Don't shoot yourself in the foot!" "Shoot me an email."
- "You're killin' me!" "You're a real buzz kill." "Don't go postal!"

- "Shoot! I made a mistake." "Bite the bullet." "Just shoot me now."
- "Let's pull the trigger." "You dodged a bullet that time!"
- "You're on target!" "Bullet statements."

After sharing these he said, **"I know it may seem like a little thing, but it's a starting point of change."**

Culture-Climate

Tony briefly mentioned that four years earlier the district had initiated the Positive Behavioral Interventions and Supports (PBIS) program, which other states such as Wisconsin and Massachusetts have initiated. Because of its focus on the positive it was a bit easier for everyone to focus on the positive after the shooting. Tony said, **"Culture is all about mission statements, posters, procedures and protocols. Climate is all about relationships and making those relationships strong and healthy by focusing on the positive we all have to offer."** Research (Steele & Malchiodi, 2012) also shows that those traumatized children who do better than other traumatized children exposed to the same situation has a great deal to do with the quality of relationships they have with their primary care takers. (Susan Connelly tells us some of the ways they do this at their school in Chapter Four.) From an administrative perspective and a trauma-informed perspective, focusing on building relationships became very critical to their recovery and healing. Tony provided several examples.

The Newtown Prevention Council

One of the examples of the importance of relationships was the redevelopment of the Newtown Prevention Council (NPC). In previous years the council kind of died out until Tony, Judith Blanchard, the district health coordinator, and remaining NPC members decided to bring some life back into it because it was too important to lose as a resource. It was originally supported by the Substance Abuse and Mental Health Services Administration (SAMHSA) grant for the prevention of alcohol abuse. They expanded the focus, so prior to the shooting they had a number of students, social workers, law enforcement personnel and a host of other agency representatives actively involved in the council. It became a close-knit community that became a tremendous resource after the shooting. When the shooting took place Tony said, "Our relationships truly made a difference in being able to respond quickly afterwards, getting people the help they needed as quickly as possible."

Reaction

Lesson

Lesson: This speaks to the recommendation in Chapter One **about establishing countywide trauma-informed task groups to create a safety net of services for the wide range of people that can be devastated by a traumatic incident.**

School Liaison

Tony talked about how he was the school liaison with the Newtown Rotary Club. That relationship he said led to the Rotary creating the first foundation for Sandy Hook in a matter of days. Within a couple of weeks it was surpassing $600,000 in donations from around the world. Because of this relationship, members of Rotary International contributed a great deal. **Establishing and sustaining relationships prior to a crisis matters immensely in a crisis.**

Schools Emergency Response to Violence (SERV)

The school district was awarded a four-year SERV grant for $1.3 million by demonstrating the working relationships they have with organizations throughout the community. Normally this grant covers a period of 18 months. It was approved with a provision for an extension of another four years in recognition that the surviving first graders were going to be impacted for many years. **Developing community relationships before a** tragedy happens certainly matters a great deal when attempting to heal and recover as quickly as possible.

Storytelling

Tony learned that storytelling is a pathway to post-traumatic growth. Tony tells several stories about his healing journey, which also addresses what he calls *synchronicity,* **meaning that connections are important and things happen for a reason.** He learned about *synchronicity* from Joseph Jaworski's book *Synchronicity: The Inner Path of Leadership* (1998). In this book, the author, a corporate business lawyer, takes us on a journey of personal insights as he describes a string of circumstances that create a unique path and put him in touch with the right people at pivotal moments in his life.

TLC Training

Tony has been at Newtown Schools for 15 years. Susan, his middle school counselor, was hired during that time. Tony remembers approving her request to attend the National Institute for Trauma and Loss in Children's (TLC) trauma certification training years before the shooting. He told us that he still has and was thankful to have the folder of information she brought back with her. **"So here we are years later with a connection that started much earlier. That's synchronicity,"** he said. **Trauma training does make a difference.**

Character Attributes—The Tree

Prior to the shooting, the school district started stressing character attributes. This grew out of the district strategic planning process prior to the tragedy. As a way to involve the entire community in supporting these attributes they used a tree to help display the attributes. They placed the tree on their website and had business size cards printed with the tree and additional information about the attributes. It was brought to Tony's attention that a 10-year-old girl in California went to the Newtown school website, copied the tree, put it on t-shirts and sold them to raise money for the Sandy Hook fund. Again he said, **"Things happen for a reason. Connections are important."**

The attributes include perseverance, citizenship, trustworthiness, responsibility, respect and caring. The last four attributes are displayed in the branches of the tree. The trunk reflects citizenship and the root system reflects perseverance. They are described as follows:

- Perseverance is working hard to set and achieve goals, learning from failure and following through with commitment.
- Citizenship is contributing to the greater good of the community, staying informed, voting and caring about school, local, state and global communities.
- Trustworthiness means being reliable, being honest, keeping promises and doing the right thing.
- Responsibility is taking control of your actions and your obligations, having a sense of duty to fulfill task with reliability, dependability and commitment to doing your best, thinking before you act and considering the consequences.
- Respect is accepting differences, using good manners and dealing peacefully with anger, insults and disagreements.
- Caring is being interested, concerned or empathetic about someone or something and expressing gratitude, kindness, compassion and forgiveness in order to help people in need.

What Doesn't Kill Us

Tony found the book *What Doesn't Kill Us: The New Psychology of Posttraumatic Growth* (Joseph, 2011), which addresses the new psychology of post-traumatic growth. He said he has read it five times since what happened and each time a bit more stuck. It really talks about how important it is to stay focused on the positives. Tony admitted that, "this is sometimes hard in my role as an administrator. When people ask me to be truthful as to how I'm doing and I tell them I'm not great, I hear this inner voice saying, I'm not doing my job right because I supposed to hide this. From a positive perspective I now am able to say to myself that this is leaking out for a reason."

Reaction

Lesson

Lesson: Although not directly stated, openness gives others the permission to be open, and being open can relieve stress and generate support. In addition, openness by leaders shows others that it is not necessary to hide everything in order to be an effective leader. In my experience working with survivors following a crisis, those in crisis trust those they feel share their worries, fears and uncertainties. They are more likely to accept and follow that person's directives, than those of people who are less open and who are perceived to not be experiencing what they are experiencing.

My Son's Graduation

Tony's son graduated from the Naval Training Academy in Chicago a few months after the shooting. He and his wife were scheduled to leave for his graduation on a Thursday flight. Tony hadn't seen his son for some time and with all that had happened, he looked forward to getting away for a celebration. On that Wednesday night, one of their students committed suicide. Tony went to school at 6am Thursday morning to meet with the Crisis Team and was able to catch a flight out that Thursday afternoon. However, when they landed in Chicago his son's girlfriend was not there to meet them. Tony got a text message that she was with his son at the hospital. He was okay but very sick. At first, he was overwhelmed with emotions and then just started laughing hysterically. When his wife asked if he was okay, he said to her, "When does it stop?"

Reaction

Lesson: At the time of this writing, one year had passed for the people at Newtown. I guarantee you **many of the staff are also wondering** *when the crises they are now experiencing because of all that happened will stop.* This is the *new normal.* Many of the stories presented in this text show, that **in the midst of one crisis, we can anticipate other crises. It really dictates that school systems provide numerous resources for staff to help them engage regularly in self-care.** It really means creating a climate where staff and students both feel comforted. (Susan will talk about acts of kindness in Chapter Four as a way to self-regulate stressful periods.) **Although not found in most plans, there ought to be in every crisis plan a plan that details the resources that are to be made available to staff along with activities in their schools that provide support, comfort and help in regulating their reactions for many months afterward.** All of this can be planned in advance. Finally, for Tony laughter was a release. Others in the same situation may need help with the feeling of helplessness such a situation can create.

On the way to the hospital Tony told his wife they needed to turn this into a positive experience. As it turned out, they were able to spend more time with their son in the hospital than had the graduation gone as planned. They spent Thursday night, the day on Friday and Saturday morning before leaving. Again he said, "Things happen for a reason."

Sandy Hook's Principal

Dawn Hochsprung was Tony's mentor as an administrator back in 1999. Tony had spent 20 years as a teacher and had additional administrative experiences in other districts. When she was hired as principal at Sandy Hook their relationship grew stronger. They thought very much alike and shared many school-related activities. One year while promoting reading at the school he was dressed as an astronaut and she was dressed as an alien. They enjoyed many moments like this. When he first started as an assistant principal with her, he remembered her telling him, "Your job is to keep me out of trouble because I'm going to say things I shouldn't and when I do you need to pull me back and make sure I don't get into more trouble."

He told us he plays a video in his head of some of their time together. **"I run it over and over, which I know is a problem for me and I'm working on it. However, I still think I should have been there to pull her out of trouble, because I would have been out the door before her.** My wife tells me that that's not a bad thing because I'm still there for the students. I know this but I keep hearing that voice saying, 'I should've been there.' I usually knew when she needed help by looking at her supply of Dove Chocolates she would keep by her desk. I would make sure she always had an ample supply of chocolate on hand. She did the same for me with M&M's.

"This October I needed to say goodbye to my good friend, so my wife and I drove to the cemetery to find her gravesite. We spent over an hour looking for it. It took us longer than we thought, but the moment we found it, two women also drove up to the same area presumably to visit another site. As we got ready to leave Dawn's site, these two women walked over and one said, 'I saw you at Dawn's gravesite; how do you know her?' I told her how we worked together and she said, 'I'm her mother.' We spent over an hour driving around to find Dawn's site and at that moment we meet her mother. **That was no accident. It was synchronicity.**

"I knew George, Dawn's husband. Her mother asked if George knew I was coming to the cemetery. He didn't. She told me to follow her because George would love to talk with me. For the next four hours my wife and I talked with George. That helped all of us in ways that are hard to explain in words. **Relationships matter."**

Picking Up the Pieces

In our opening remarks we responded to the statement about recovery being a marathon with the analogy of the need to be patient and to pace ourselves in order to continue to move forward to complete that marathon. Related to post-traumatic growth, which also takes time to experience and patience, Tony came across an analogy that described trauma as a broken vase and that growth is "making a stained glass out of the broken pieces."

Reaction

Lesson

Lesson: It's going to take time. This expands upon Elizabeth's comment in Chapter Two related to the importance of self-care. We've all heard the saying, "Lets pick up the pieces and move on." Unfortunately, it is not that easy. **It is going to take time to discover which pieces fit with what other pieces.** The reality is some pieces become so fragmented they just don't fit any more. The reality is in our efforts to piece our lives back together, we discover a new life, a new normal. How we look at ourselves, how we look at others and how we now look at life is through a different lens. It takes time to adjust to that new view. It takes time to feel comfortable with this new view. At the time of this writing, it has been a year since the Sandy Hook tragedy. Tony took us on his personal journey. His journey has not yet ended, but it is one that has been filled with so many learning experiences and lessons we know he has passed on to his staff and students in ways that will help all of them become more resilient. In this next section, Chapter Four, Susan Connelly, a Newtown middle school counselor, tells how she, her peers and families are piecing together their "new normal."

Newtown, Connecticut: Susan Connelly—School Counselor **4**

Susan Connelly, a Newtown Middle School counselor, like Tony, has many connections to Sandy Hook students from her 13 years in the district. She knows many of the families and parents of those who were killed. She reveals her struggles and how she continues to help others and herself. Much of what she shares are prescriptions for self-care. Many of the lessons are embedded in her comments and will be in bold print. Continuing the format in previous sections, we ask for your reactions following some of the experiences she describes.

Susan began by telling us that her comments are based solely on the experiences that she had with staff, students and parents with whom she directly interacted. She wanted us to know that they were not representative of the entire town or the entire school district. As she said, "I discovered the town and its citizens and staff members had many different kinds of reactions."

Reaction

Lesson

Lesson: This supports that there is no one intervention that fits every situation or every individual in crisis. In crisis we need to take the position of not knowing what is best for each individual. We need to remain curious so as to be able to identify the varying needs of those in crisis and what will matter most to each at that point in time. Being curious is the primary process we need to engage if we wish to determine what is going to be most helpful. Being curious means we must empower people to tell us what is and what is not helping and to respect what they tell us matters most to them. This does not preclude giving direction when that crisis is so intense that individuals are unable to effectively manage. It does not negate immediately changing what we are doing when those individuals tell us it is not helping. **We must remain flexible in our responses, because what may help one person may harm another.**

Trauma on Top of Trauma

Sandy Hook experienced a number of traumatic incidents just prior to and after the shooting. Susan told us that the shooting was not the only trauma in Newtown that year and the year that followed. Hurricane Sandy caused a good deal of anxiety in late October, as many in Connecticut were without power or lost homes, schools were closed due to power outages and the roads were blocked by fallen trees. Then in early December, two weeks before the shooting, one of the high school students was hit and killed by a truck when crossing the street. Another seventh grader was less than 3 feet behind him. She was not injured physically, but being a witness to this tragedy induced a number of reactions. Then in May, another seventh grader committed suicide. So they had one trauma on top of another. Susan said, **"We now listen with a very deep, refined filter always searching for what might not be spoken in words, but what the heart might be expressing in actions or inactions. The filter is always there, but now it's more like a coffee filter instead of a colander. It's a lot more refined.** Our teachers, secretaries, custodians, and administrators are all listening through this filter today."

Keep It Accessible

Susan's son is an Eagle Scout and has been in the Boy Scouts for many years. We all know their motto is *Be Prepared.* She acknowledged that we can't always be prepared for every single problematic situation or emergency but, as she indicated, "If we're as prepared as possible, we're better equipped to handle the challenges that come our way and decrease the negative impact that trauma can have on all of us." As Tony told us earlier, Susan received her Certification as a Trauma Specialist from TLC 10 years earlier. She too indicated that when the shootings took place, she returned to the notebook that she brought back with her and gave Dr. Salvatore. She said, **"It gave me a starting point as to what I could do immediately and what I needed to be considering weeks and months later. I am so thankful I had it available."**

Having a Plan

She went on to tell us that, when Hurricane Sandy hit the coast two months prior to the shooting at Sandy Hook, being prepared meant stocking up on water, batteries, food and boarding up windows. **"Being prepared for a crisis,"** she said, **"also means having a plan and ensuring that everyone who is involved in that plan is aware of the protocol, is practicing those protocols and has good communication and input into that plan."** She said that it's very important that we know our resources especially in an emergency. She said she has learned **"to hope for the best, plan for the worst."**

Reaction

Lesson

Lesson: In planning for the worst, we can arrive at a more realistic understanding of the many responses and strategies needed during and after a crisis by examining possible scenarios and introducing a long list of questions beginning with "What if . . . ?" These questions need to be directed at all the components of that crisis. *What ifs* cover the actions, timing, responses and needs of parents, students or clients, staff, administration, school boards, law enforcement, first responders, media, community leaders and politicians. (A comprehensive listing of *What if* questions can be found in the Appendix. The list is also an excellent tool for evaluating preparedness.)

When presenting to crisis teams, I will review their protocols and address those areas that need adjusting. **However, even the most comprehensive manual is of no use if you do not have access to it.** I always ask team members how many carry their manual with them in their cars. Very few do and experience repeatedly demonstrates that team members do not always have access to the manuals they keep somewhere in the facility. If you recall, several of the responders in New York did not have their manual with them when the chaos ensued. In that chaos it was very difficult to remember what needed to be done to deescalate the many situations they faced.

When entering into a crisis as a responder, you want to do so at a cognitive level, in your thinking brain, not your emotional midbrain. This helps prevent you from being overwhelmed by what you may experience when you walk into that situation. Law enforcement, firemen and other rescue workers are trained to be purposeful and thoughtful in the many decisions they need to make quickly. If as a crisis team member you are called to respond, simply looking quickly at your protocol manual for those briefly listed procedures you are to follow in the many situations you may encounter allows you to be moving into that situation in a more structured, orderly fashion, being proactive rather than reactive.

Stay Connected

Tony told us earlier how important it is to stay connected to our resources. "As a counselor," Susan said, "I already knew who the professionals were in town, but I didn't know if they were trauma certified or not. I didn't know their connections with psychiatrists. I knew my psychiatrist, but who was connected with them was really important in getting people help as quickly as possible. **We now have a comprehensive list. If we had that list beforehand, it would have saved a tremendous amount of time and energy and decreased the frustration of the parents we were trying to refer after the shooting."**

Keep Staff Informed

Susan said she's had to remind staff many times of grief and trauma responses and not to assume that people are going to remember. She's asked them to keep these posted and accessible. She also asked others to be her observers as to how other staff were doing, especially the bus drivers, custodians, cafeteria workers, administrators, teachers, paraprofessionals, library staff—anyone who has contact with the students. **"It is very important," she said, "to monitor each other as the healing process continues."**

Be Kind

A quote from Dawn Hochsprung, the principal at Sandy Hook Elementary, has been placed on every school bus in Newtown reading**, "Be nice to each other. It's really all that matters."** Susan went on to say, "We shouldn't need reminders to be kind, but we do. Kindness takes all sorts of forms, a smile, letting someone pull ahead of us when were stopped at a traffic light, holding the door open for more than one person, sending a letter the old-fashioned way. All of these are quite simple yet we get so busy in our lives that we forget."

   "When we do kind acts for other people, it really increases our well-being and it decreases our stress. I think Robert Fulghum (1999) really missed this one of his lists of *All I Really Need to Know, I Learned in Kindergarten*. Kindness should be the very first thing on his list. It's not on that list at all. I was shocked when I saw that. In our town, acts of kindness have spread like wildfire over the past 11 months."

Reaction

Lesson

Lesson: A trauma-informed environment will promote the value of generosity and provide the opportunities for traumatized children to learn and feel the benefits of being generous. The value of generosity or "the quality of being kind" (Merriam-Webster Online Dictionary, n.d.) actually has biological and psychological reparative value that benefits traumatized children. Zak, Stanton and Ahmadi (2007) present a neuroscience perspective that the experience of generosity releases the hormone oxytocin. Oxytocin actually calms the brain and creates trust, which facilitates bonding with others (Carter, 2007; Ratey, 2002); in traumatized children, trust is frequently absent as a result of broken attachments. When people reach out to others, negative emotions such as hostility, resentment and fear become displaced by positive emotions.

Be Grateful

Susan told us that it really helped her to focus everyday on what she needed to be grateful for, but that she had to be reminded at one point to begin to do this. "There were a few of weeks," she said, "when I was just overwhelmingly sad. My older, wiser sister called me and said to me basically, if you're having a bad day ask yourself what you are grateful for today. I asked her what she meant. My sister told me to think. You should be **starting every day and ending every day with exactly what you're grateful for because that's where your focus will be brought back to every time you need support.**"

Choices

"I recognize," Susan said, "there are days that are very challenging in everybody's life. Some days I just want to get home, curl up and forget the entire day ever happened. We certainly have had a few of those since all this happened. The fact is we have so many things that can bring us comfort and help us regulate our reactions. **But again, when we are under a good deal of stress, we sometimes need to be reminded to choose those things that have brought us relief in the past.** For some, their selections may be limited because they simply have not focused on their well-being, on stress management."

She went on to present a long list of activities she and her colleagues were practicing. As she was running through her list, I had to say to myself there really is no excuse for us, as professionals, not to be taking better care of ourselves. Her list included: "Reiki, yoga, faith, a bubble bath, time with the kids, time without the kids, reading, fires in the fire pit underneath the stars, being with our pets, kayaking, comedy movies, compassionate acts, journaling, being honest with ourselves when we need to take more breaks at work, meditating. There's also play, music, making jewelry, shopping but not spending, cleaning or not worrying about keeping the house clean, gardening. We can go to church more, travel out of town more, not read e-mails before going to bed, play more board games with the family, write poems, go dancing, jog, go to therapy and get some help from melatonin and Xanax."

Reaction

Lesson

Lesson: If we are not engaged in good self-care as a weekly routine, we are not likely to immediately engage self-care actions when under stress. In fact stress often drives people to work harder, not less, when self-care has not been part of their weekly lives. Susan told us we all have plenty of choices, but **the lesson here is that many will need a nudge, a reminder. It helps, in intense crisis situations involving many victims, when schools can integrate self-care activities into the daily schedules and the community can support victims by offering a variety of activities.**

Community Support

Newtown businesses provided educators and family with tremendous support. Graceful Planet is the yoga studio in town and they offered six months of free yoga classes for the staff in the district. They were jammed. Newtown Youth Academy is a sports arena in town. They encouraged kids and adults to get out and get moving and helped by offering free classes for them. They brought in people from all kinds of college teams to work with the kids and to inspire them to get out and move. The Sandy Hook Run took place in January. They never expected it to be as big as it was. It was to raise money for the families. There were teachers' unions from across the country there. "I talked to teachers," she said, "from Texas, Maryland and Boston, who came to run this race and show their support for all of us."

Accentuate the Positive

We all know that if we only focus on the negative we're going to miss the opportunities to see all those wonderful things that are happening around us. People suffered a great loss in Newtown on December 14. There is no discounting that and the great loss that people continue to feel in the community. But life has also been brought back into town as well. Susan told us that in her middle school they had six births. She quickly added, "not in school itself, but staff members who had six brand-new babies. There was the joy of going to their showers and there was also the joy when two staff members got married."

Mentioning these positive moments was an introduction to describing their support of PBIS, which Tony had mentioned earlier. She told us that they were in their fourth year of PBIS at the middle school and one of the things they began two years ago was having the staff members acknowledge positive things that the children were doing in a more public way. She said, "We have four principles, Be Positive, Be Safe, Be Respectful and Be Responsible. When staff observe students exemplifying one of these four characteristics, they give them 'shout out' cards. Students bring their cards to myself, or one of the counseling office secretaries. We then put them up on the board. The kids can see them, the parents can see them and other staff members can see them."

"At the end of the month we pull them all down and sit the kids on our long stairway. We take their picture, which goes into the Newtown newspaper and then the fun really begins. We throw all the names in a box and then we pick five 7th graders names and five 8th graders names by random. Those 10 children then get a catered lunch by one of our local restaurants. They love it because they get to eat in the conference room on the roller chairs. Kids never get to go into the conference room so we end up having *rolling chair wars* and they really truly love it. It's so special."

```
Reaction


```

```
Lesson



```

Lesson: PBIS brings about a wonderfully positive cultural and climate change in schools for most students. However, **it is important to remember the earlier lesson that "no one intervention fits every child."** PBIS does not necessarily help traumatized students because engaging in behaviors to be rewarded can present a significant challenge to these children. Today neuroscience has confirmed that trauma is experienced in the midbrain, the limbic region, sometimes referred to as the "feeling" brain or the "survival" brain, where there is no reason, logic nor language. Reason, logic and the use of language to make sense of what has happened are upper brain-cognitive functions and become difficult to access in trauma (Steele & Kuban, 2013; Levine & Kline, 2008; Perry, 2009). Reason and logic are often dominated by the emotional brains of traumatized children. Principal Silvia Cordero of Eldorado Elementary School says these children slip through the PBIS and restorative practices nets because "without a trauma lens, we miss components about what makes these approaches work or not work" (Ellen, 2014). Today's crisis team members must not only be trauma informed but skilled in trauma-informed practices. Furthermore, schools need to consider incorporating programs, such as PBIS, within a trauma-informed framework.

Be Thankful for Gifts Large and Small

Susan decided to tell us about a few of the gifts they received. After she shares a few of these stories we will ask for your reaction and the lesson that emerges for you. She began with, "We had 60,000 teddy bears all shapes and sizes. We didn't of course use all of them, so a lot of the teddy bears were then disseminated to the communities that we knew needed them. And then there was Ben's Bells. The bell started showing up around town. The mission of Ben's Bells is to inspire, educate and motivate each other to realize the impact of intentional kindness and to empower individuals to act according to that awareness. Ben's Bells started in Tucson, Arizona, when an artist's 3-year-old child suddenly passed away and she needed to reach out for ways to help her family heal and the community around her to heal. These bells are wind chimes made out of clay and then painted. They're beautiful."

Nickel Mines School

The day before she was ready to leave school to travel to see us she found five packages on her office couch. She told us that, ". . . the secretary didn't know what they were, but they had my name on them. I opened one box and pulled out a beautiful hand-painted ornament that had the picture of one of the Sandy Hook children with her name on the back of it who had been shot last year. There was a letter in the box. These boxes had come from Nickel Mines Amish School in Pennsylvania. They had a shooting October 2, 2006 (Amish School Shooting, n.d.). Ten girls were held hostage and then five of them were brutally murdered. The ornaments came from one of the students at Nickel Mines. **The love and the amount of time that had to be spent putting these together for the Sandy Hook victim's families over the last 11 months was heartfelt."**

Impossible but True

About four months before she visited with us, Susan went to the central office to look through all the cards that had been sent to Newtown. The central office had sent a message to everyone to come take a look at the cards and if they found a card that *spoke to them* to take it with them. She told us that that she had never seen so many cards in her life. There were boxes filled with cards that children made from all over the country. She told us that when she opened the very first box of the hundreds that were there, she put her hand in and pulled out a green card. It was from Chardon High School, who also had a shooting one year ago. "Out of those boxes," she said, "I picked this one card and today two of the counselors from Chardon are sitting next to me. Amazing." (We will read about their experiences shortly.) The card read,

> *"Stay strong. We know how it feels. Our school had a shooting too. We're so sorry."*

"Things like this," she said, "let us know how connected we really are, how things happen for a reason, as Tony said earlier, and how important these connections are to healing."

Snowflake Central

A blizzard of snowflakes was sent to Newtown. The National PTA had put out a request to send snowflakes to Sandy Hook so they could decorate their hallways. Susan said, "I had the honor of going to a warehouse we called *snowflake central*, to help unpack all these boxes of snowflakes. We kept the letters and where the snowflakes were sent from so we could later thank them. The joke the next day was we knew who had been to *snowflake central*, because inevitably there was a piece of glitter caught somewhere on their body. They were beautiful, very creative and just heartwarming. Every school had snowflakes up. When Sandy Hook moved to Chalk Hill School, they had them lining the hallways and in the classrooms. **They were just surrounded by this flurry of love.** It was quite a sight."

Reaction

Lesson

Lesson: If we pause for a moment and review these recent stories, we realize she is describing **the power of sensory interventions,** meaning all the visual symbols of love, care and support surrounding people every day: Ben's Bells, the snowflakes, teddy bears and cards. The thousands of gifts sent did create a challenge when it came to storage and paying for that storage, but they **conveyed and accomplished what words alone could not.**

Another Kind of Help

"We had counselors come from all over who were available 24 hours a day, during Christmas vacation and New Year's Eve. We were so grateful," she said. "They had families and jobs that they gave up to come and help us."

Reaction

Lesson

Lesson: The importance of having help was actually stated very well by Fred Rogers.

> When I was a boy and I would see scary things in the news, my mother would say to me, "Look for the helpers. You will always find people who are helping." To this day, especially in times of "disaster," I remember my mother's words and I am always comforted by realizing that there are still so many helpers—so many caring people in this world.
>
> (Huffington Post Parents, 2013)

The Dogs

"There were also a dozen therapy dogs. They were awesome. But also, when help from others was not helping, the dogs did. Now being a gracious hostess we had to have dog bones for the dogs, because you can't give them cookies, coffee, cake or bagels. So we still have bones for the dogs for when they come back."

```
┌─────────────────────────────────────────────────────────┐
│                                                           │
│  Reaction                                                 │
│                                                           │
│                                                           │
│                                                           │
└─────────────────────────────────────────────────────────┘

┌─────────────────────────────────────────────────────────┐
│                                                           │
│  Lesson                                                   │
│                                                           │
│                                                           │
│                                                           │
│                                                           │
└─────────────────────────────────────────────────────────┘
```

Lesson: Over the last 25 years research shows the physical and mental health benefits of living with a pet. Pets help lower blood pressure, lessen anxiety and boost our immunity (Davis, 2013). We also know that therapy dogs affect the release of various neurotransmitters in the brain. A pet also increases the production of oxytocin, which is heavily linked with bonding, while lowering cortisol levels associated with stress (Therapy Dog, 2013). There are numerous heartwarming stories of the emotional benefits of therapy dogs for children and adults alike. Many states now use therapy dogs in schools, courtrooms, juvenile facilities and prisons. The *Journal of Personality and Social Psychology* reported that dogs can provide the same emotional benefits as humans (Montimurri & Braiser, 2013).

Create

Susan told us that this past summer she had attended the TLC Summer Assembly and a workshop on journaling. Participants in the workshop were asked to create an ABC poem. She said at first she thought to herself, "How in the world am I'm going to do this, but it flowed." This is her poem.

> *Am I to Believe That I Can Heal? Decidedly, yes. Each day I will find opportunities to grow, to heal, to share my insights, or to just gain knowledge, always remembering that my base is my love. Maybe by my nurturing and guiding others they will discover answers to their questions and I to my own. I am resilient. I am strong. There is a path before me. It is filled with unknown wonders,*

visible and invisible. Where it goes is to be explored, bringing me strength, confidence, and knowledge from yesterday and today and forward to tomorrow. I will be zealous in my pursuit of peace.

Reaction

Lesson

Lesson: It is the creative process that matters, not necessarily the shape or form of what we might create. Creating is a process of discovering. As we discover whatever emerges, we are empowered. Being empowered makes it a bit easier to manage our fears and anxieties.

Mindful Activities

Susan said that she never saw herself as the yoga type. She said that she was a triathlete, enjoyed swimming, biking, and running, but never thought of yoga as something to be enjoyed. **But for her yoga became her *coping buddy*.** In the first year following all that happened, it helped her learn to lead her body through some of those most difficult challenges. She said, "It won't bring back the 20 children and my six colleagues, whom I remember every day, but being at peace allows me to get through each day. It helps me to focus on working with the students, who themselves are struggling with the ongoing effects of this horrible trauma. It helps me to guide parents and staff, who at times are lost and overwhelmed as well. **This doesn't mean I don't lose it. I've had my days, but going back to breathing and yoga puts me back in the moment and helps me get through that moment.**"

Create a Calm and Peaceful Environment

Susan gave us a brief description of her office. "The harsh, fluorescent lights are never on in my office. Actually they have been off for years because they gave me headaches. What I find is that four soft general lights help to reduce the intensity and the duration of emotional responses for anybody who comes into my office. Music also helps." She mentioned that YouTube has a host of guided meditations, as does iTunes, which can be downloaded onto phones and MP3s for easy access throughout the day. "It's very common," she said, "to have people come in and say can I just sit here for a minute." However, she told us, "If running a marathon, hiking a mountain or paddling a kayak is how we find peace, then it is not important how you seek it."

Random Acts of Hugging (RAH)

Susan also practices random acts of hugging (RAH) in her family. She said, "I'll look at my 16-year-old son and say 'RAH'. He'll come over and give me a big hug."

Laughter

She asked us how many of us remembered watching the *I Love Lucy Show* as Lucy stuffed her mouth with chocolates, because the conveyor belt was going too fast. She told us that when her son asked her what she wanted for Christmas last year, she told him to get something that's going to make her laugh. He got her the first season of the *Big Bang Theory*, which is one of her favorite shows. She said she sat and watched hours and hours and laughed to the point of crying. She said it was wonderful. She also told us that one of her students walked in to her office one day and said she needed her computer. She asked why and the student replied that she needed to go to YouTube. So she pulled up YouTube and she found funny cat and dog videos. Susan said she never laughed so hard with a student like that before. **It was hysterical. She said, "My secretary came in wondering what we are doing and then she started laughing and before we knew it, we had a room filled with people laughing at these silly videos."** She said she learned from her son about Vine, an instant streaming video site of short clips that are very funny. She said they are also very silly but they're very funny. **Laughter is a great therapy**.

Don't Let Them Suck Your Fun Circuits Dry

Susan ended with this final story. Anna Grace Marquez-Green was one of the victims of Sandy Hook. Her mother told the following story. "I was kind of sad a few days before the shooting and when my daughter saw me she asked me what was wrong. I told her that work was a little bit difficult and made me sad. My daughter then turned to me and said, mom don't let them suck your fun circuits dry." **Sometimes wisdom comes from the youngest of children**.

The loss of life at Chardon High School in Ohio on February 27, 2012, is our next story as it is connected to the unlikely experience described by Susan about pulling one card from thousands of cards that happen to be from students in Chardon, Ohio. I also spent time with responders in the Chardon community and asked if they would be interested in sharing their stories with a larger audience totally unaware of Susan's experience. It is a small world. The magnitude of what happened at Chardon is far smaller yet the pain and issues Chardon survivors and responders experienced were as challenging as those faced by the survivors and responders from our other stories. And, as is always the case, new lessons were discovered.

Chardon, Ohio: February 27, 2012   **5**

In Chardon, Ohio, on February 27, 2012, sophomore T. J. Lane pulled out a gun. He shot and killed three students and wounded two others in the school cafeteria. One was left permanently paralyzed.

Chardon is a small town with a population of approximately 5,200 people living in a 4.6 square mile area. The high school has 1,100 students. The school cafeteria is the meeting place for students waiting for buses to take them to other area schools. It is a large cafeteria that left hundreds exposed to possible death that day. Being witnesses, the lives of many students and their families were altered forever. For example, one mother was on the phone with her daughter, who was in the cafeteria during the shooting. Her mother was powerless to do anything to protect her daughter. She was not alone with this intense fear and overwhelming sense of powerlessness. One student, who knew those who were shot, did not want to return to school and his mother was now asking what she should do. Many middle school students also had connections to the victims, which added to the number of students and families impacted by this violent trauma. The safety of this small community was shattered that day.

Laura Serazin and Misty Ramos, mental health practitioners from Cornerstone of Hope located in a suburb of Cleveland several miles from Chardon, were one of the agencies that responded to Chardon's needs. Although they provided assistance immediately following the shooting, the experiences they share are unique. Following the initial psychological first aid that was provided after the shooting, the school attempted to return to routine as much as possible. It was hoped that the summer break would allow people to move forward. However, there was concern that there would be some families and students who would be anxious about returning to school given all that they had experienced. Laura and Misty's story is related to meeting with these families and students prior to the start of the following school year. The outcomes were quite revealing. They serve as a blueprint for others working with small groups of families concerned about safety and security following violent incidents.

Community Support

Before reviewing their experiences, it is important to know that Chardon had no crisis team prior to the shooting. It had to rely on outside help. As can be expected some of the help was beneficial, some of it was not. It is understandable that in this situation recovery was less than structured. They learned numerous valuable lessons and will be better prepared in the event of future crisis. Fortunately, they had immediate community support and resources, which the United Way managed. They coordinated bringing a variety of different agencies and professionals together to provide psychological first aid and crisis intervention. This added to some of the chaos because a previously prepared recovery plan was not already in place. However, it did provide the students, staff and families with a number of resources.

The United Way immediately established the Chardon Healing Fund to provide support for the families of those children who died and were injured. The fund provided assistance to meet the basic needs of the families, covered the financial costs families incurred and provided a vehicle for the student who was permanently paralyzed. It also provided for a Resource Officer, a strategic planning committee and ongoing wellness programs. These programs included service projects like *Project Linus*, which provided blankets, dog leashes for therapy dogs and "service days" for students to perform various services in the community. It also supported *Education Nights* for the community to answer questions and provide additional emotional support. All of this was of tremendous help in the absence of a formal school crisis team.

"We Know the Future Will Be Hard"

As it was in Sandy Hook and so many other communities, the outpouring of community support was invaluable and critically important to recovery for the Chardon community. Benjamin Harvey, a sophomore from a neighboring school, wrote the poem *Chardon High*, one of several gracing the walls of Chardon High today. He writes about the sudden loss of friends, the tears that were cried, the prayers everyone sent and the hope that their futures will be better protected (Boyle, 2012):

> *February 27, 2012. On a quiet Monday morning, on a hilltop that stands high, terror struck without warning, the kids of Chardon high. That day we lost too many friends, and uncounted tears were cried, all her strength and love we send the kids of Chardon high. We know the future will be hard, and we pray that through the sky, 1,000 angels will fly to guard our brothers and sisters at Chardon High.*

What to Do With the Cafeteria?

As was mentioned earlier, resources were provided to assemble professionals from a variety of agencies. Each had their personal opinion of what was needed. One of these was to redo the cafeteria and rearrange the tables where the students were killed. It was all repainted. When the students returned they let it be known that they didn't like what was done with the seating. They returned the seating to the way it had been for years.

Reaction

Lesson

Lesson: Memorials have been discussed throughout the text. **What emerges is the importance of taking time to discuss the options with those who must return to the site of that tragedy on a daily basis. These are the individuals who matter the most. Although not everyone will be satisfied by the final decisions, their input is critical to identifying**

the possible solutions and arriving at an informed decision the majority can accept.

Preparing to Return to School

Whether it is several days, weeks or months later, the return to school involved in a violent trauma will need to be addressed with those most exposed to that situation. Prior to the Chardon High School reopening in September after the summer break, Cornerstone of Hope in partnership with Chardon Schools advertised the opportunity for families and students to come together to address and hopefully resolve whatever anxiety, worries or concerns they had about returning to school. They indicated that their objectives were to create a safe opportunity for families and students to express and find relief from their concerns, worries and reactions; to communicate their specific needs to the school if desired; to connect with one another as survivors and for the entire experience to be a positive one to help them discover their strength and resilience.

The families of the students who were victims and witnesses to the shooting attended. One of the families came with 12 family members. There was a mother, who was also a middle school teacher, who attended because her daughter was in the cafeteria during the shooting. She also brought her other two daughters. Another mother and her son who were very close to the victims attended. Four groups were established. The family with 12 members was broken into two groups. Seven students were in their own group and the remaining group consisted of six parents. Besides Laura and Misty there were trained facilitators for each group. Three major activities were scheduled. All participants participated together in a *drumming circle*. This activity was followed by a *safety island* activity that participants worked on in their individual groups. This was followed by lunch. The final activity focused on honoring those who died.

Releasing-Empowering-Unifying: The Drum Circle

The people who participated brought a diverse range of reactions. One woman cried for quite some time. She was like a "well of emotions." Others were angry and still others fearful. Some were quiet and some, especially the students, who were there because their parents brought them, were initially quiet and seemed disinterested. Understandably, everyone was a bit reluctant and worried about saying too much or the wrong thing. They worried about losing control of their emotions, and worried about what others might think about them. It was important to give them a vehicle to alleviate some of this anxiety and to help them discover they could express their emotions safely in a nonthreatening atmosphere while learning the benefit of self-regulation. It was also important to begin with an activity that was empowering while also fun. It was decided to use an activity involving drums. Everyone participated as an entire group.

People were asked to identify what they were feeling and then to drum that emotion. The other group members repeated what they heard, joining together to echo and validate that person's emotion. Some volunteered to talk about the emotion they were drumming and received feedback from the other members in a group. Often they expressed similar reactions. This began the normalizing of one another's diverse reactions. The sound of the drums that morning gave everyone a way to express themselves without having to rely on the limitations of language. It discharged the physiological manifestations of their many emotions, worries and fears and unified the entire group—children and adults alike.

Reaction

Lesson

Lesson: Biofeedback studies show that drumming along with our own heartbeat alters brain wave patterns. It soothes, calms, regulates and allows for self-expression without words (Payne, 2014). Drumming the sound of what they may not have the words to express or are afraid to express verbally, especially in a group setting, accomplishes this. It also induces harmony among its participants, which in this case was essential for all the participants.

Safety

The next activity was designed to identify the subjective level of safety participants were experiencing. It also was designed to help families discover what matters most to them as a family and as individual members of that family. It helped them to define the kind of environment that will best support their needs and the values and beliefs that support the behaviors of all in that family. Everyone was provided glue sticks, construction paper, miniatures, animals they selected to be a part of their community or family and other materials to create their own island. They were instructed to give their island a name and a motto. They needed to determine what they might do if their safety was threatened and list the rules of the island. Later they were also asked why they selected the animals they did. The students worked in their own group; the extended family members composed two groups; parents made up the fourth group.

Tropical Ski Island

(The two extended family member groups' islands are described in this and the next section. The opportunity to write your reactions and the lessons that emerge follow these descriptions.) The one extended family group named their island after one of the children who died. They asked that we not identify the child by name. The island was called . . .'s *Tropical Ski Island*. One rule they had was that there must be compassion on their island. There could be no hatred or anger, no cell phones or Wi-Fi and no fast food. Their motto was "hakuna matata," which means no worries. Their sign was the Circle of Life. They had many paths on their island and each path was identified by a name. The paths were named "love, compassion, peace, spirit and hope." These were the paths that people who visited their island would take to come into their community. If something were to threaten the safety of the island, everyone would come together at the center of the island to stay safe. Their strength was being together as a community.

Paradise Island and Serenity Island

The other extended family member group called their island *Paradise Island*. There were no weapons, no violence, no anger and no sadness. Their motto was, "Welcome to our peaceful island." Their song was "Don't worry. Be happy."

The parents' island was called *Serenity*. There was to be a positive attitude at all times, no drama. Their motto was "We have many parts, but just one body." Their song was also "Don't worry. Be happy." Because this was *Serenity Island* the only visitors they allowed were those they trusted. Visitors needed to have background checks and they needed to know the purpose of the visit. They also needed to take a lie detector test so that they knew they were telling the truth. There was also a Navy Seal base under the water.

At one point people were asked why they chose the animal that they did. A mother, who was the middle school teacher, chose an elephant. She said, "I feel I have to be strong for my kids but I also have to be gentle, caring and nurturing." The conflict she expressed was that because she did not lose a child, she almost felt like she shouldn't be feeling the way she was feeling. The group was very supportive of her. One of the parents, whose child died, selected a tiger. The tiger brought protection because, as this one father said, "This is never going to happen to another one of my children." There was a zebra for diversity and loving everyone. Another person selected the phoenix. She said, "The Phoenix will rise from the devastation. We shall survive."

Reaction

Lesson

Lesson: This activity teaches us far more than asking participants directly about their safety concerns. The activity was structured in a way to allow participants to think about how best to use the resources they were provided, including one another. It also helped to display the extent of their need for safety (lie detectors, underground Navy Seal Base, etc.). It demonstrated the many methods and, for some, the limited methods they chose to protect themselves. It also clearly communicated what mattered most to them at this point in time.

Group Differences

There were some interesting differences between the parent groups and the student group that Laura and Misty shared with us. In the parent groups everyone worked together. They also helped each other with the construction. On the other hand, the students, who interestingly called their own island *America*, worked individually and very quietly. Each selected their own piece of the island to create their safe place. They did not work together. The adults planned and worked together. The students surrounded themselves with many barriers for protection from outsiders but also from one another. One student created a completely self-contained environment so he could survive on his own. Another child had an underground shelter where he kept all his food and could be safe in the face of danger. The animal he selected was a dragon, which provided even greater protection. All of the students perched their animals in safe places high above while "on watch" yet isolated from one another. The adults basically worked together as a unit to protect the entire island, whereas the students were just protecting themselves individually.

Reaction

Lesson

Lesson: The subjective ways children experience their lives are dramatically communicated not through language and not always through behaviors, but by engaging them in activities that are structured to reveal the ways they now see and experience themselves and their world as a result of their exposure to trauma. It is important to keep in mind that the surviving children's parents were attempting to cope with the tragic love loss in their lives. As a result, their children's world became even more stressful. Not only were they attempting to cope with fears about their own safety following the shooting, they also were now trying to cope with the worries and anxieties caused by their parents' reactions to this tragedy.

The children's need for a sense of protection is well documented by the ways they barricaded themselves on their island. At first it was thought that children were disinterested but observations are often misleading. What is revealing is how alone and disconnected they are on the island they call "America." Their isolation and limited coping skills leave them quite vulnerable. **The research is quite clear that those who do better than others exposed to the same tragic situation have a significant connection or attachment with a significant adult in their lives (Steele & Malchiodi, 2012). For these children the focus on connection must become the focus of intervention. It is critical to their resilience at school and at home in everyday life, which will certainly present them with additional crises.**

Transition Back to School

Laura and Misty used this activity to help parents and students talk about their worries and concerns about going back to school. The parents started talking first and really focused on the need for protection. They said, "We need bars on the windows and metal detectors at all the entrances. We may need to make sure that nobody gets in without an identification badge." They also said that the cafeteria should not be a bustling hub for other students. It was felt that, "If the other students, like the shooter, had not been there waiting for their buses, this would never have happened." Most interesting was the response from the boy, who didn't want to go back to school and who had been pretty quiet throughout the day. He said, "Wait you can't keep us in a bubble. We have to be able to live. You can't just lock us up and put bars on the windows. If you put bars on the windows and something happens we can't jump out the window. We're locked in that room. You have to change people." This was quite profound and symbolized on the children's island by their choice of perched and flying animals.

Reaction

Lesson

Lesson: Feeling safe is not just about creating a physically safe environment. Physical safety measures may slow down those wanting to do bodily harm, but may also increase the risk for death when those efforts do not provide for easy escape for potential victims. In Chapter One, we described the response of staff to having resource officers in their facility after a student killed one of the staff. They too understood that **having a sense of safety is also about feeling connected, trusting those in their environment and having open communication about their concerns.** The island the students created had no such connections, trust or communication among those on the island. This must also be the focus of creating safe school environments.

Paying Tribute: Memory Stones

Lunch was relaxing and a fun time. By this time, much of the initial anxiety, the crying and other reactions had significantly diminished. People were laughing and having fun. The last part of the day was designed to help channel those unwanted reactions into a positive resource. This activity allowed for a final expression of all their reactions resulting from this violent trauma that took the lives of friends, families and children. It also allowed them to put their shattered feelings, memories and dreams back together but in a way that focused on the valued memory of each of these children. It was designed to empower the participants to discover a new strength-based, resilient memory of loved ones and cherished friends.

Each person was given a ceramic plate and permanent markers. Each was asked to write down an emotion that they were still holding onto. They could also write down the dreams they felt were now broken and shattered. They then put the ceramic plate into a pillowcase. Each was given a hammer and instructed to break the ceramic plates into pieces. The pillowcase kept the ceramic plates from shattering into pieces all over the floor. This was important because the pieces would become a resource for rebuilding their memories of all that happened and what they experienced. Amazingly, the student, who spoke up about the adult recommendation to put bars on the window, asked if he could take his pillowcase outside. He was followed outside where there was a large cement patio. He then took the pillowcase and with all his might repeatedly smashed it against the cement patio. He pretty much shattered the pillowcase, while releasing a tremendous amount of energy.

After he returned to the group, everyone was asked to take all their broken pieces and make something new and beautiful. This would be their tribute to their friend or loved one. When finished, many wrote the names of their loved one on their new creation. They took these with them as a way to remember the value that their loved ones and friends had brought into their lives. The participants indicated that they were leaving feeling and thinking much differently than when they first arrived.

Reaction

Lesson

Lesson: What they created had a unique meaning for each. What they were learning was that their shattered lives can be transformed. Safely discharging powerful emotions and being actively involved in re-creating the personal and meaningful memory of their friends and loved ones gave them a sense of strength to move forward.

Staff Wellness

A similar day was held for staff. During this in-service day a number of presenters were invited to the school to conduct a variety of presentations and workshops. As an aside, what was interesting was that as a number of staff responded to the day by saying that they preferred not to have the kind of workshops that they had previously. Many of them wanted to move beyond what had happened and not be reminded by workshops because it implied they still needed to deal with what happened. Laura and Misty did an art-therapy-based workshop focusing on relaxation and guided imagery to regulate their stress, fears, worries and anxieties. They called it "A Pocket Full of Relaxation." First they were engaged in muscle relaxation and then guided imagery. The guided imagery activities were about creating a visual journey to their "safe place," a place to go during difficult times to regulate their reactions to difficult experiences.

Following the presentation of different guided images, each person was given a wallet size card. They were given art materials and asked to create a collage to reflect the imagery that was most calming and helpful for them. The references they chose were related to family, friends, community and spiritual aspects. They could then choose to keep this card with them as a quick reference when they needed to spend a few minutes in their safe place to regulate their reactions to a stressful situation. The cards were laminated for protection. One teacher stated she would keep the card in her

> **Reaction**

> **Lesson**

desk drawer. Another laughed and responded, "Mine will be right on top of my desk."

Lesson: Guided imagery, meditation, yoga and many other mindfulness activities are known to help reduce physiological and psychological reactions to difficult times, as well as to regulate reactions to stressful situations. They can be very empowering. Regulation is important because

it is the core of resilience and the management of the intense reactions
induced by trauma.

Memorial Service: One Year Later

In Chardon there is a large town square where the students had gathered
after the shooting. For the one-year anniversary, they wanted to walk hand-
in-hand from the school to the square and have a memorial ceremony at
the square where students, who wished, could convey their stories and messages to those in attendance. Others did not want to attend this memorial.
Because there was such a diversity of opinions and because some people
wished not to continue activities that were related to what happened, the
school provided multiple opportunities for people to do what they needed
to do that day.

They published a memorial book that was in full color. It had the photos
of the students who died and highlighted their lives and the different events
that they had experienced. For some it was a wonderful keepsake that focused
on the positive memories of their classmates. For others it was a reminder
of the lives that were lost, the violence in society, the loss of what was once
thought to be a safe community. Students also showed a video, shown in the
library, to pay tribute to the victims and to the staff members they felt were
also heroes that day.

The following year a meeting was held to discuss the two-year anniversary.
While discussing the plan, several people mentioned that they wondered if
the first-year Memorial was really helpful because it was the day after that the
"shooter" pleaded guilty. They thought that the second-year Memorial should
be the same as the first year so people, who felt cheated out of the intended
value of that first memorial service, had another opportunity to honor those
whose lives were ended. Some thought that the service should be all week
and filled with numerous community activities. What they decided to do was
to go ahead and have a memorial for those who wanted to have a memorial
service, but also present others the opportunity to focus on future wellness
by providing optional activities for them. **Presenting choices became very
important.**

Laura and Misty learned several lessons from their unique involvement
and observations.

• Not having a crisis team and a structured recovery plan in place created a
  number of challenges that could have been prevented.

- Having prior experiences with or knowledge of those who are asked to help is critical to avoiding additional crises that can arise when relying on those who are not known to the team. This is critical for maintaining safety standards and quality of care.
- Giving people multiple options to do what they feel is most helpful for them is essential.
- Appreciating that in-school violence is traumatic for some but not for everyone is essential.
- Understanding how violence can shatter one's sense of safety is as essential as providing those who struggle the most with safety the opportunity to find ways to manage their reactions.
- When events in school happen prior to summer break, there are those who will be concerned with returning to school and families who will be equally concerned about allowing their children to return to that environment.
- Involving everyone with multiple opportunities to discuss what they believe can be most helpful is essential to building a compassionate community and arriving at solutions that are supported by the majority of those most impacted by that incident.
- Finally, when working with those who are the most exposed and who continue to have reactions and concerns in the months that follow, engaging them in structured activities that have multiple purposes is far more beneficial and healing than direct verbal interventions.

Laura and Misty's experiences support the value of intervening with adult survivors (family members) as well as students. Our final story is about the recovery efforts following the deadly shooting at Virginia Tech. The student population is comprised of adults. Although the recovery efforts described supported the recovery and well-being of this adult population, they are efforts that should be integrated into recovery efforts in K–12 schools. As with the previous experiences, there are unique lessons that were learned. Their approach to the on-campus memorial, the focus on highlighting their long-standing values and the approach to helping students during the summer, when they returned to their home state, were quite unique.

Virginia Polytechnic Institute and State University (Virginia Tech): April 16, 2007

6

On April 16, 2007, Seung-Hui Cho, a senior Korean American student shot and killed 32 Virginia Tech students; 23 additional students were injured and of those 17 were shot. Before the day ended, he took his own life. Virginia Tech is located in Blacksburg, Virginia, a town of 46,000. There are 30,000 students who attend the University. Dr. Gerard Lawson, associate professor of counselor education at the University, was directly involved in immediate and long-term recovery of the students, their families and the community. The lessons he has learned over the past seven years remain very pertinent to having a well-prepared recovery plan for incidents involving single or multiple victims, either at the university level or at the K–12 levels. The comments presented in this text are not reflective of the University, nor of the administration, but specifically of his own experiences. He began by saying that, "Even though we are in a business where words and language are our stock and trade, I do not have words to explain what happened on April 16th. I can't make sense of that. I'm not sure that I ever will. When a very troubled young man ends the lives of thirty-two people there is no way to make sense of it. All I know is that the world is a poorer place without them in it. These were remarkable artists, and scholars, athletes and citizens that would've changed the world."

Responding to Media

There were numerous headlines in newspapers around the country that referred to the "bloodbath" and "massacre" at Virginia Tech. It was described in one paper as a "bloody campus" and the question of where were the warnings was asked repeatedly. Dr. Lawson said, "That's not what we were asking that day." He told us that he saw a number of students approached by reporters saying, "Don't you think someone needs to be held responsible? Don't you think that someone needs to be held accountable?" He was present when they approached the president of the Student Government Association and was concerned about how this young student might respond. However, what he said was part of what set the model for the rest of the way they moved through this tragic situation. What he said when asked if he thought someone should be accountable, was, "What we really need are candles. Virginia Tech is having a candlelight vigil tonight and Blacksburg is out of candles, so what we need are candles." Dr. Lawson said that he did not believe that this student recognized what he said at the time. What he was saying was that, "We need light in this time of darkness. We need to see the path forward."

Reaction

Lesson

Lesson: Dr. Lawson told us that the headline in the student newspaper the following day was not about bloodshed or massacre, it was about "Heartache: Our Sorrow and Resolve." "The truth was," he said, "that we were talking about how to support our community. We were asking how do we get help to the people that need help; how do we give them what they need and how do we find the people that feel disconnected from the community and get them reconnected." **In this day of social media, those in charge can quickly present a response that is prepared well before crises occur. That response can be crafted to keep the focus on what is being done to move forward, on the strength and resilience of those involved and the values they work hard to uphold. Such a quick response can help combat the negativity, accusations and blame that may come from other sources.**

The media, as in so many similar situations, was shameful. Some were sending interns in with a nametag that said *family member* on it trying to get information about the families. He said when he was leaving one evening, he came around the corner to the front doors and stopped short because he saw a semicircle of reporters with cameras waiting outside the door. They wanted to snap the picture of everybody they could. One of the state troopers was standing there and asked him if he was okay. He wasn't quite sure how to answer, but he didn't want to have to go through that crowd of reporters. The state trooper sensed this and walked out with him telling the reporters to make room. They all did put their cameras down.

Reaction

Lesson

Lesson: It is critical to know beforehand what the city, county and state law enforcement departments are able to do to help manage the media. Keep in mind that in some cases there may be dual departments involved. This can be planned well in advance. Do keep in mind that, because of staff changes and possible changes in procedures, it is critical to meet at least once a year with law enforcement to review the extent of their help in a crisis.

Students

Virginia Tech made the decision to follow their students closely, to do the heavy lifting for them while allowing them to guide the response around the issue of memorials, the day of remembrance and all of the things that followed from that point forward. They communicated to all the students that they could ask for help for whatever their reasons were at the time. They communicated that they did not want the students to get into thinking that they were not quite as bad off as others and avoid seeing a counselor. There were hundreds of professional counselors whom the University had invited to assist with students when they returned to classes. Counselors were identified clearly with purple armbands so those seeking help would know who to go to directly. They also instructed the Employee Assistance Program (EAP) counselors, coming in from all over, that they were to meet with anyone walking through their door. Using EAP counselors is a benefit of insurance. Many of those seeking help did not have such insurance coverage. The university did not want to have people turned away because they did not have insurance. To the credit of the EAP counselors, they agreed. **The extent of the resources provided to students, families and staff at a time of crisis is obviously important. As insurance becomes more of an issue in this country, establishing the extent of services in a crisis that providers are willing to support at no cost becomes important to the well-being of the entire immediate community.**

Attending Classes

The shooting occurred on April 16, a few weeks before the end of the semester. One of the things that happened immediately was the President of the University decided the students could go home if they wanted to. They were presented with three ways they could end the semester: They could take their current grade and leave immediately. They could negotiate with the professor one or two other assignments or projects and complete those at home. If they already had something under way and they wanted to be able see that through they could negotiate with the professor as to when they needed to submit their work in order to finish out the semester. It was all entirely up to the students to manage and select what they wanted to do. Dr. Lawson said that this was an incredibly good idea. He mentioned that he had 30 students but his friends and colleagues, for example, in the sociology department, have 600 students in one class. The staff went out of their way to accommodate their students. Supporting them was a priority. Interestingly, most of the students could have left but most of them stayed. A number of students did go home for a day or two and then came back to finish the semester. The message to the students from the director of the University's counseling center, Chris Flynn, was, **"If you want to stay here or go home, go where you get the best hugs."**

Reaction

Lesson

Lesson: School schedules are planned well in advance. From this per-spective, critical periods in a schedule can be very easy to identify. Should a crisis occur during one of those periods, the specific resources or choices that might be needed can be planned for ahead of time. For example, 9/11 happened shortly after the beginning of school, in the midst of still adjusting to all the issues that emerge at the beginning of a school year. Virginia Tech happened near the end of the school term and close to grad-uation and the summer break for many. This created differently unique challenges.

Returning to Classes

Before students returned to class, the office ran the schedules for every student who was injured or killed and for the shooter, so they knew where those indi-viduals would have been for every class throughout the day. When students got back to their classes, they arranged for two counselors in every room with students that would have been affected by the shooting. The response was pretty unpredictable. Counselors would be in one class and assume that they would have the teacher's support to spend time with the class, but get a response of, "You can leave the paperwork, but we have an exam to take." They would have a different response in other classes whose teachers gave them the entire class time to sit and talk with the students. They also initially had counselors in the dining halls and would get reports back that no one would make eye contact with them. They removed the counselors because it was felt that people just wanted to eat in peace. However, the next day they

heard from the staff who were working in the dining halls that they were having difficulty because of all the students who were coming through their lines
in tears. They didn't know what to do for them. Different days presented very
different needs in terms of our response. "Basically," Dr. Lawson said, "we
just took our lead from how others responded to us."

Reaction

Lesson

Lesson: In crisis, leadership certainly needs to initially decide what might
be helpful. Hopefully, the choices are previously identified. At the same time
it is critical to remain flexible by having multiple responses available. If one
response is not working, it needs to be replaced with yet another response
until those in crisis let us know that what we are doing now is most helpful.
**The lesson we learn here is to listen, observe and respond to what mat-
ters most to those who are in crisis at that point in time. However, it's
also important to keep in mind that what we might do one day may not
be helpful on another day.**

When School Was Not in Session

Dr. Lawson said he was in contact with the American Counseling Association (ACA). There was concern for students' well-being during the summer
while off campus. This was difficult for staff as well, because they would not
be able to see students and check on them as they did normally when on
campus. He said he wanted to be sure they had support if needed. At first
ACA thought Dr. Lawson was referring to his 30 students. When they called
back to clarify, they learned he was referring to all 30,000 students. The ACA

said, without missing a beat, that they could find support. They sent notices to all 50,000 members to identify those who were agreeable to offering five free counseling sessions to Virginia Tech students asking for help. From across the country, 700 counselors signed up to help. About 170 students used this resource. More important than the number who participated was the fact that the University was able to send 50,000 students an email saying, we are concerned that you are okay, and here are some resources if you need them.

Reaction

Lesson

Lesson: Having strong relationships with service providers who can also quickly mobilize multiple resources is critical to the well-being of all involved. This also addresses a question many schools ask as to what their response should be when crises happen during the summer months. The answer to this is to open your doors to the community as a place where they can gather for support and help from counselors. This will also tend to minimize unwanted responses and reactions when students return to school after the summer break.

Families

When families began to arrive on campus they were directed to the far end of the campus. Some of the families were able to reconnect with their sons or daughters almost immediately. There were a number of family members who had been trying to contact their son or daughter by cell phone. However, the cell phone towers were overwhelmed by the volume of phone calls in and out of Blacksburg, so that became problematic. It certainly increased their worst fears. The other problem was that the students who were actually indoors in Norris Hall, where 30 students were killed, did not take anything with them when they were evacuated. They didn't have their cell phones, so those phones were ringing in an empty building. Some of these students' parents were fortunate to quickly find that their son or daughter was okay, that they were with a friend and just not connected to their cell phones. Other families had to be redirected to the hospital, because their son or daughter had been injured.

The families of the students who were killed had to wait to find out what actually happened with their child. The state police chaplaincy services were utilized to assist in death notifications that day. They began to work with some of these families before the formal identification was actually made. The identification process did not happen immediately. "This was the hardest part of what we did," Dr. Lawson told us. "It was also painfully hard for everyone involved because it was such a protracted process. It's not like at all what happens on television," he told us. "Before parents could be brought to identify their child, the medical examiner's office needed DNA evidence, fingerprints or dental records to verify the identity of each student who was killed. Family members were only able to identify their child after this was completed. What prolonged this was the fact that Southwest Virginia has only one medical examiner. That examiner sees maybe 1 or 2 homicides a year and that day there were 33, so the examiner's office was backed up for four or five days before they made those final identifications."

Reaction

Lesson

Lesson: To plan appropriately, know beforehand the procedures related to the medical examiner authorizing confirmation of the victim by a loved one or family. Furthermore, being trained to assist with death notification, or at least to be aware of the process and what is communicated to loved ones and families ought to be part of crisis team member training. Using this information, team members can identify what role they might play to further support families at the time of notification.

Self-Care

Dr. Lawson told us that before the shootings most of his research was about counselor wellness and counselor impairment issues. He was involved in identifying what was needed to stay well and to avoid burnout, compassion fatigue and vicarious trauma. The immediate response around campus was to turn off the television. That happened within 5 hours of the shootings. He told us that he no longer watches television coverage of traumatic events if he can at all avoid it. "The reason for this," he said is, "You can't always trust the information presented."

A Community Effort

It is very important that leadership in a crisis be previously identified. Equally important is that the leadership is driven by very clear objectives. At Virginia Tech a mental health advisory group was established immediately. Members of that group included the director and staff of the counseling center on campus, Dr. Lawson, colleagues, staff from the counselor education program, the marriage and family therapy program, psychological services, human resources and the counselor from the on-campus EAP. The international student services group was also involved because the shooter was a Korean American. They thought it was important to be sure that they were including the international community in their discussions, to better plan for how to meet the needs of this community.

There were a couple of things that took place that were quite interesting. When the Governor declared the area a state of emergency, the Community Services Board, by law, is in charge of the mental health needs of the area. This included Virginia Tech. As soon as the declaration was made, the director of the board called and asked us what we needed. "To their credit," Dr. Lawson told us, "they could've very easily come in and said they were in charge, but instead they really became a partner with us."

Reaction

Lesson

Lesson: We've repeated many times over how important relationships are to recovery. This is no different regarding the training of crisis team members in the district. When working with school districts around developing crisis teams, we always recommend that at least two people from each school be involved in the training. The purpose for this is to ensure that when a crisis occurs at one of the district schools, the staff will have received the same training as the district team members. This is important because we want those staff at that school to be in a leadership role and to direct district-wide team members that may come to assist. These two staff members are more likely to know their students and staff best and, therefore, will have a better understanding of the priorities needed at that point in time. They will also be able to quickly identify those students or staff who may need immediate attention. Additional challenges are created when designated school personnel, from each school in the district, have not been trained in crisis protocol and responses. When the district team arrives at these schools, what they are prepared to do may conflict with the unique needs of the school as well as its administration. **Administrators will be far more comfortable when leadership comes from their own staff members.**

A Trauma-Informed Approach

Dr. Lawson stated, "the first thing that was decided was that there was not going to be a meltdown." He said, "that they knew their campus better than anyone else. And because they were counselors they also knew the research. They knew that throughout a lifetime 80 to 90% of people are going to have some experience that will qualify for PTSD, but the lifetime occurrence of PTSD is only in the 9 to 12% range. The idea that everybody was going to suddenly develop PTSD," Dr. Lawson said, "was just a fantasy that was not going to happen."

Reaction

Lesson

Lesson: We certainly do not want to make the assumption that, just because a number of people have been exposed to the same trauma, they all need the same help. We want to have time-specific interventions that begin with the least intrusive and only move to more intensive interventions when survivors display, by their behaviors and reactions, they are in need of more intense interventions. Psychological First Aid and crisis intervention are those interventions that are best suited to be offered immediately, as well as over the next several days. For those who need additional support, intervention needs to be more focused on their unique needs. And should reactions continue six to eight weeks beyond that period, additional trauma specific intervention is likely needed. (Examples of time-specific interventions are provided in the Appendix.)

The Virginia Tech Motto

Virginia Tech's motto is *Ut Prosim*—"That I may serve." Adhering to this motto, staff began to think about how they were going to weave service into the recovery process. They asked themselves what people needed to do. Dr. Lawson said that in these situations, "People need to take action of some sort to feel engaged in the recovery process, to be part of the solution as well as the healing."

A Value-Driven Campus

Virginia Tech began as a military institution so the campus still has the drill field where the Corps of Cadets do their drills to this day. On campus is a War Memorial Chapel. In this area are inscribed the names of all the Virginia Tech students who died in service to their country, and those who earned the Medal of Honor. The pillars on either side of this area are known as pylons. On each of the pylons is also inscribed the characteristics of the Virginia Tech student. These include brotherhood, service, sacrifice, leadership, loyalty, duty, honor, and *Ut Prosim* ("That I may serve"). Interestingly at Virginia Tech every classroom has these values posted for everyone to see. "It was these values," Dr. Lawson indicated, that "became the guide for how we were going to reestablish the identity of our campus, rather than allowing others (the media) to define it for us."

Reaction

Lesson

Lesson: In reality how many schools actually have a motto that exemplifies their overall purpose? In reality how many schools look to their values as critical to driving the recovery process? In many cases staff when asked cannot identify their values. It was Virginia Tech's motto and values that strengthened and hastened their recovery.

Discovering Their Resilience

Every third state trooper in Virginia was sent to Blacksburg. The sense of safety was reinforced by the visible police presence. However, actions were needed to also help everyone deal with the inner sense of safety they were robbed of that day at gunpoint. One of the things staff did immediately was to pass out material about the normal responses to trauma so people had a benchmark they could look at and say, "I'm doing okay and my friends are doing okay." They also used the *Victim to Survivor to Thriver* diagram developed by Dr. Lennis Echterling of James Madison University in Virginia. Dr. Echterling's crisis intervention model addresses making contact, making meaning, managing emotions, finding resolve and resolution to move from being a victim to being a survivor and a thriver (Echterling and Presbury, 2004). They used this diagram to be sure they were incorporating into their recovery plan the transitions from victim to survivor and thriver. He said, "We began working on this immediately the morning of the 17th. We understood that we could not rush people into a thriving state, but were going to provide them multiple opportunities to discover their resilience and ability to thrive despite all that happened."

Convocation

The convocation was held at 1pm on April 17. It was the first community-wide healing process since the shooting. It was held in the Coliseum, which holds 19,000 people. The President of the United States was there along with the Governor. "However, the most important person there from my perspective," Dr. Lawson told us, "was Nikki Giovanni." Nikki Giovanni is a Poet Laureate and outspoken advocate for social justice issues. "What was amazing," Dr. Lawson said, "is that she had less than 24 hours to come up with something to say to the entire world about what just happened. She delivered the convocation address that spoke to our emotion, but also our hopefulness in a way that was compassionate and reflected the resilience of our campus community." Her address (Giovanni, 2007) began:

> We are sad today, and we will be sad for quite a while . . . We are brave enough to bend to cry, and we are sad enough to know that we must laugh again. We are Virginia Tech . . .

She continues to mention situations throughout the world where people who did not deserve to lose their lives. She describes Virginia Tech students as being open to the possibilities "to invent the future" despite their tears, sadness and disbelief. She closes with, *"We are the Hokies. We will prevail. We are Virginia Tech."*

You are encouraged to read and listen to her entire speech. It is quite moving and captures the inner resilience we all hope will be available to us under such tragic situations. What made it so moving was the fact that it reflected the values and character of the school itself.

Following her speech applause went on for quite some time and then resulted in the chant of "Let's go Hokies. Let's go Hokies." At that moment recovery began. "In essence," Dr. Lawson said, "she was speaking our language, reminding us who we are, our resilience, our resolve and ability to move forward."

Reaction

Lesson

Lesson: (In my opinion) the recovery process of Virginia Tech, driven by its focus on community, its values and motto, not only accelerated recovery but protected its staff, students and families from secondary wounding and prolonged pain. Furthermore, it allowed them to define to the world who they were as a community and a university, rather than allowing others, like the media, to define them.

Memorials

There were a number of impromptu memorials that were made almost immediately. One of these included 33 Hokie stones that were placed in a semicircle on the drill field. Later the original stones were replaced with engraved Hokie stones for each student killed. The Hokie stone is a material used in the construction of almost every building on campus. Virginia Tech owns the quarry where they are mined so at least the façade of almost every building has the Hokie stone. The morning after the shootings, they began to show up on the drill field. There was one for each of the victims including the shooter. Interestingly, Dr. Lawson told us, "that one got stolen every night and every morning the next day was replaced until finally the woman, who was putting the stones out, wrote a column in our campus paper. She basically wrote that she could continue to replace the stolen stone and thought it was important to recognize he was the 33rd victim." That stone is not included in the permanent memorial.

Dr. Lawson said they broke a number of rules with the Memorial because, "We listened to the students and not the research." He said they put the memorial right in the middle of the drill field by the review stands. He said, "You normally don't want a permanent memorial right in the middle of an area like that. However, it became a rallying point for people." **Similar to the listing on campus of those who died in the war and earned the Medal of Honor, and the pylons inscribed with their values, this memorial became another symbol of their relentless spirit, their courage to move forward and their determination to never forget.**

The Need to Do Something

Another interesting story he shared was about the drill team conducting a 24-hour candlelight vigil for the victims of the shooting. One of the victims had been a member of the Corps of Cadets, which is a civilian Corps of Cadets but they do everything in military style. The Corps took great care to be sure that this was handled in a way that is consistent with military honors. Anyone who has ever been in the presence of *Echo Taps* knows it's a very emotional time. What they also wanted to do was to honor the victims by burning a candle for 24 hours and to have Honor Guards standing by that candle throughout those 24 hours. A number of volunteers were needed to do two-hour shifts. **They had so many volunteers they had to make the shifts 15 minutes, so everyone who volunteered was able to serve as an honor guard.**

Making Meaning

In addition to creating a memorial that visibly displays the resolve and resilience of Virginia Tech and its students, it was important to offer ways for people to make meaning of what had happened. Making meaning out of a crisis is about discovering our resilience, our inner ability to thrive despite the crises in our lives. The way they helped people on campus was by putting up

4 × 8 whiteboards all around campus for people to be able to write what they needed to write. Students, as well as visitors, could write down their thoughts and comments about what this experience meant for them. For people to be able to express themselves and what they were experiencing is part of making meaning of such a tragic situation. Dr. Lawson said they eventually had to move all these boards indoors and that they are now, along with hundreds of thousands of cards, in a storage facility they had to rent to be able to store all the materials.

Reaction

Lesson

Lesson: Giving people opportunities to do something in a crisis is empowering. Using a visual medium for people to express themselves in writing was a wonderful way to help them express the meaning this had for them as individuals. **It gave them a sense of empowerment, a voice in their community. It also allowed them to know that there is no one right way to think or feel although many do experience similar thoughts and feelings.**

Cultural Sensitivity and Responsibility

Dr. Lawson mentioned that most on campus knew, at some level, that the Korean culture is a very collective culture. The statement that reflects this is, "If one of us has injured you, we have all injured you." Because the shooter was Korean, they heard stories from around campus about a young Korean lady who was going door-to-door in her apartment complex, knocking on doors and apologizing. They would get calls from people asking what was going on because they didn't understand the cultural aspect of her behavior. Another interesting factor was that the Korean Student Association began meeting regularly trying to figure out how best to manage what happened, and to support one another. At one of their meetings, the Saudi Arabian Student Association came to them and said, "We've been where you are. After 9/11 we were where you are now and we know what it feels like to think that everybody is looking at you and blaming you." Together they arranged a bowling tournament for their two groups to go out together and support one another. These are not groups you would normally think of hanging out together. However, they became a tremendous support for one another through this period time. "So again," Dr. Lawson said, **"When you let students do what they need to do, they find artful ways to take care one another."**

The Power of Music

If you recall, Dr. Salvatore introduced us to the concept of synchronicity—nothing happens by accident. Dr. Lawson gave us another wonderful example. His wife is a professional musician with the Richmond Symphony. On the night of the shootings they had one of their Masterworks concerts. That day they changed the program and put on the *Enigma Variations*, which is the piece that was played, for example, at John F. Kennedy's funeral. It is a regular piece in times of mourning. This is a very emotional piece of music that was played emotionally that night by the symphony. What Dr. Lawson did not realize at the time was the meaning it was going to have for him several days later.

A few days later he said he felt the need to check in with the school band to make sure they were doing okay. They were going to be performing for everyone. He realized that one of the students who died had been a musician with the band and another was part of the marching band. He said he should have known that they were going to be affected, but it wasn't until he got there that he really got in touch with how much they were affected. He said he was able to speak to this group of mostly 18-year-olds about the power of what they do and the power of music to heal because of the concert he had heard his wife play earlier. **He described to the band how the professional musicians at the Masterworks concert were playing the *Enigma Variations* (2014) and were weeping as they played because of the moving power of their own**

music. The band director got up and said that they had a choice and that everyone would understand if they wanted to cancel their performance. All the members said that they wanted to play. They played beautifully.

Some of the band members used their music to lift the spirit of those who were injured, even before this happened. Some of the wounded students were taken to the regional hospital, while some others were taken to trauma centers further away. Without telling anybody, the Marching Virginians, the school band, went and performed in the parking lots of the hospitals. They performed the Hokie Pokey and just about everything else played at their football games. **The students who were recovering were at their windows feeling the power of the music to lift their spirits and to let them know they were not alone or forgotten.**

Connections

The many stories Dr. Lawson shared with us speak to the importance of connections. Many of the actions Virginia Tech was able to initiate were as a result of the many connections they had with the larger community.

Lesson: We never know what kind of connections or relationships may be the most helpful. Listening for connections that may be significant for each survivor and trying to support the facilitation of that connection can be as healing as any formal intervention process.

Heroes

The police were on campus three minutes after getting the call for help. Dr. Lawson told us that for him the police were heroes. They put their bodies in between the shooter and the students who were running out of Norris Hall. The campus also has a Rescue Squad, which is entirely student-run. On the day of the shootings, there was not one person who died after the rescue squad arrived to attend to their injuries. This was difficult for them because they were attending to classmates and friends, fraternity brothers and sorority sisters. They were tending to their own and they certainly were heroes as well. He also told us that there was a professor in the Engineering Department who was shot to death holding the door of his classroom closed so the students could escape out the window. None of them were injured by gunfire. "He too is a hero," said Dr. Lawson.

Final Words

Dr. Lawson's final words to us were, "There is no disputing that these individuals, who did what they had to do under horrific circumstances, are heroes and that they acted heroically. And it takes nothing away from them, when I also say that as I speak to you as a group of counselors, I know I am in the company of heroes. As counselors you choose to meet with people when they are in pain and facing life's challenges. It can take a toll on you through burnout, compassion fatigue, and vicarious traumatization. **You need to be sure to take care of yourselves, to remain vital in this work, because you do make a difference in the lives of those individuals you meet.**"

What If . . . ?   **7**

Following is a sampling of the hundreds of *What if* questions I've been asked over
the years by educators and community responders assisting in the aftermath of
school tragedies. As community responders assisting schools, it is important to
appreciate the unique challenges schools face that determine interventions that
are, in many cases, different from those that are initiated for trauma incidents
not involving schools. When crisis teams meet to review possible scenarios asking *What if* questions is a process that helps to develop contingency strategies
and the protocols needed to be prepared for these contingencies. These *What
if* questions help to identify the many possibilities that can arise following a
crisis. They address some of the challenges others were not prepared for when
they happened. General comments will be made regarding the different themes
that these questions present, such as managing parents. Keep in mind that each
school and school district is unique. What may be an appropriate protocol for
some may need adjusting for others because of the unique elements of the district, its families, students and community. Although many school districts have
crisis teams, levels of preparedness differ. These questions reflect the information and training many teams today need even though standard protocols for
many of these situations are well established.

How to Use

Use the following questions to help examine:

- What you might change or add to your current plan to respond to this
  particular concern;

- What resources are needed to support your responses to the possible situations that can take place;
- What possible roadblocks you might anticipate in initiating the protocols in question; and
- What additional information would help you (such as reading, training, reviewing, communicating) so that you can address each *What if* possibility more effectively.

Parents

What if parents are demanding the release of their children from school?
What if parents do penetrate the building in a crisis situation?
What if parents are flooding into the school for information?

Standard safety protocol should address how parents are to be contained outside the school as well as inside the school. In a lockdown situation parents need to be directed to a site outside the school. Assigned staff should be immediately deployed to this area. Hopefully a strong relationship has been established with local authorities so they can assist with managing parents in this contained area.

The protocol should also address the strategy for an organized reuniting of students with parents. It should also address the method for accounting for the well-being of all students and the appropriate formal release of students to parents. In releasing students to parents it is very important that parents provide appropriate identification. In elementary schools a crisis is a time when noncustodial parents have attempted to take (kidnap) their child.

Following a lockdown parents should not have access inside the building until it has been formally secured. Once secured, parents should be escorted to a contained area and not allowed to seek out their children. The children are to be brought to them in an organized fashion and the appropriate release form signed before that child is released.

A large-scale disaster can necessitate an immediate evacuation, as was the case in New York on 9/11. Remember, that concerned for the safety of the children, some parents asked to take several students with them because they lived in the same area. A release form can be prepared ahead of time for this possibility. Also remember that the other issue in that situation was that children were released to the first parent able to get to the school. When the other parent arrived for their child, the staff could not tell them where the other spouse took their child. As a result staff began to ask the parent where they were taking their son or daughter so, if the other spouse arrived, they could provide them with that information. This is one of those contingencies many plans do not address.

What if parents come in and create a disruption?
What if there are many parents coming into the school who are hysterical and creating more hysteria with the student?

Disruptive parents must be attended to immediately. A crisis does not give parents the right to be disruptive or engage in behaviors that are frightening and disruptive to others. Others will not mind if police are asked to assist in this situation. Clearly protocol must be clear as to the ways disruptive parents can be best managed. If this takes place inside the school, staff should be ready to quickly escort parents to a contained area away from students. If parents are being contained in an outside area, definitely ask police to manage this situation. This can become a crowd control issue especially at such an emotional time.

It is recommended that several crisis team members be identified who have experience and a comfort level working with upset and irate parents. It is also important to respect gender issues. When addressing upset parents it is best that a female and a male staff person do so together. This helps prevent further escalation of adults who may have issues with one specific gender. Working in a team is also good mental health for those staff exposed to what can be a potentially volatile, even dangerous situation.

What if the family of a student who has died does not want information shared with the student body and faculty?

Some parents do not want schools to share information about what happened to their child when death occurs outside of school hours. Unfortunately, in today's social media world, students will be texting one another immediately a great deal of information, which is often inaccurate and misleading. It is important to address with students whatever issues may be emerging as a result of the student's death. It is important in today's world to also educate children about the hurt and pain they can cause others and themselves by what they communicate.

It is also equally important to respect the family's wishes as best possible. Representatives should meet with family members to inform them that information is already being communicated about their child. Your hope is that they will allow you to provide correct information. In the case of death, once the medical examiner office actually confirms the death, it becomes public information. Communicating information that has not been confirmed can increase vulnerability to legal action by families. Be certain that your protocols clearly address the legal issues involved in sharing information before that death is officially confirmed.

Once the medical examiner's office confirms the death and associated details, it becomes public information. At this point schools certainly are able to discuss or answer children's questions about those details. In situations where death or cause of death has not been officially confirmed, yet students are communicating what they believe happened, it is helpful to refocus them. By this we mean indicating to them that formal confirmation of what happened has not yet been made available so it's really not possible to talk about some of the details of what happened. However, what is important is that their classmate or peer is no longer going to be a part of their lives. This is sad and at a time like this it helps to talk about what everyone remembers most about that classmate/friend.

What if a student dies (murdered) and the mother/father wants to speak with the students the next day or two?

In situations where grieving parents want to talk to their child's class, thank them for being concerned but do not allow them to do so. The emotional state of survivors, so close to the death of their child, is unpredictable and can be frightening and overwhelming for children. Often the parents need to talk with their children's friends or classmates is out of the need to make sure that their child is remembered in a positive way.

Do let parents know you do appreciate their concern that their child's classmates remember and talk about the good things about their son or daughter. Do ask parents what they want their child's classmates to remember about their child and indicate that you will convey the message to them. If they still question why they cannot meet with the class, simply indicate that experience has shown that once with classmates, so soon after a tragic loss, survivors have understandably become so emotionally overwhelmed they are unable to continue or frighten the children by their emotions.

What if students are saying the death of their peer was a suicide, but the parent/family does not want the school community/children to know?

Students will use social media immediately. Even when that child's death may be questionable, but students are communicating it was a suicide, it is best that schools meet with students. There are some legal issues involved.

It is critical not to refer to the death as a suicide until the medical examiner's office confirms that death as a suicide. Even though students may know it was a suicide because their peer was verbally talking about it, schools face liability issues if they speak of it as a suicide before the official confirmation has been made. Understandably, some examiners may rule the death accidental in order to protect families from the stigma of suicide.

If students are saying that their classmate or friend talked about taking their life, it is important to redirect them. Indicate that there is no official word and that what is more important than the cause of death is the fact that their classmate / good friend is no longer a part of their lives. Keep the focus on the reactions they are having to such a loss, but also take the opportunity to educate them to what to do and what to say if they have a friend who is talking about suicide.

What if the parents do not take a child threatening suicide seriously and do not pursue mental health help? Child Protective Services (CPS) does not always follow up; often the parents expect the school to take care of it.

There are some situations that limit what we can do. If a parent of a potentially suicidal child refuses recommendations for help, there is the legal responsibility of informing CPS. As reported by many across the country, CPS may offer little support. As long as the student has not been disruptive in the school environment, schools are required to allow the child to attend school. In many cases, this can be a safety net, although stressful for assigned counselors or social workers. This does go beyond protocol regarding recovery following a crisis but an issue many social workers and counselors deal with daily.

Training in suicide prevention and intervention is certainly beneficial. Schools are not treatment centers, but professionals can provide tremendous support within the limits of their professional responsibility in the school setting. Most nonfatal attempters I have met over the past 30 years report that at the time of their attempt they felt no significant connection to a significant adult in their life. It only takes a few minutes for school counselors and social workers to make and sustain that sense of connection. Given what we know about trauma today, every brief action taken to simply let students know we are thinking about them stimulates positive brain responses far easier than words alone.

What if the parent of a student dies of suicide?

When a student's parent ends their life by suicide, classmates will know and need attention. The student will need help with returning to school. His or her classmates will also need help with how to relate to that student. Further information on student reentry can be found in the Appendix.

What if we receive word that a parent dies while their child is at school and the surviving spouse wants to have their child finish the day without being told what happened until the child gets home?

If a student's parent dies while the student is at school and the family does not want the child to know until the child gets home, it is appropriate to honor the request. It may be best not to inform staff of what happened until the child leaves for home.

What if a parent enters the school and is quite angry, even irate?

This is one of those protocols addressed in most safety and security school protocols. However, safety protocols are not always communicated well to staff. Those who have the difficult challenge of meeting with angry or irate parents certainly need to know how to establish a safe environment as well as engage in safe practices with potentially volatile adults. Sitting closest to the door, while that parent or parents are on the opposite side of a fairly large table, could momentarily prevent them from reaching you should they escalate into an attempted assault, and is a well-established safety procedure. Unfortunately this and other procedures are not always followed.

Leaving the room's door ajar will allow for quicker exit if needed, as well as the opportunity for others to hear your call for help and be able to quickly scan the room before entering. There should always be backup personnel in close proximity to where you are meeting potentially violent adults. They should be aware of the possibility of having to intervene and what their responsibilities are in this situation. Having a Resource Officer nearby would be the ideal arrangement. Just seeing a Resource Officer when walking to the designated meeting area can help de-escalate confrontational behavior.

Those meeting with adults should be skilled in de-escalation practices. One way to begin to de-escalate upset adults is to acknowledge that their anger conveys how concerned they are about their child, that you respect their concerns and definitely hope to arrive at solutions as quickly as possible. Ground rules regarding behavior and language should be set immediately. If this further activates those adults, it is a signal that they may not be able to regulate themselves. Again, it is also important to have two staff people present, male and female, to minimize gender issues that may trigger that parent. In today's world, these should be concerns everyone considers when meeting with angry adults; their actions cannot be predicted.

In the majority of cases parents will not engage in assaultive behavior. In most cases school personnel are quite skilled in de-escalating difficult situations. However, what often are not practiced are the types of safety measures just cited. Some may not be aware of these, while others believe they are unnecessary. There is always that tendency to believe, "It will never happen here or to me." Having worked in the mental health field for years, it does happen even to skilled professionals. The few simple procedures mentioned earlier are designed to minimize the potential dangers when dealing with upset adults. This should certainly be a discussion among members of the crisis team and those assigned to safety protocols.

What if a parent wants to be part of a crisis response?

We do recommend that there be a parent representative on the crisis team. Parents can often provide excellent suggestions related to all of the parent issues that can take place during a crisis. However, parents should not be part of the crisis response. Emotions can run high when you believe your own child is in potential danger or are unsure whether he or she is safe. There are liability issues that the school may also face if relying upon parents to engage in tasks that are generally assigned to crisis team members.

School Staff

What if a staff member isn't dealing with the situation appropriately? What if a staff member is impacted by the crisis (related, knows student or family well, or has had recent losses), but insists on being part of the crisis team response?

As described in several of the experiences presented early in the text, staff are as vulnerable to intense reactions as are students. If staff members are having a difficult time it is appropriate for crisis team members and/or the staff's supervisor to provide them immediate attention and in some cases send them home. Staff members who are directly impacted by what has happened to a student or even another staff person should not provide direct intervention. They should be considered a victim in this situation and supported in the same way others in crisis are supported.

Some staff will be able to accept that because of their relationship with the victim or their response to what happened, they should not be providing crisis intervention. However, they may want to stay to be of help in some way. People in crisis do better when they can do something help-ful. There are a number of ways for staff to be of help without provid-ing direct intervention. They can make sure the primary responders have the resources they need, find space to meet with students, run errands, or track down team members. Making sure the team is following protocol is another important task. Supporting team members by removing them from the environment to a room where they can take a rest for 15 minutes in the morning and afternoon while snacking on protein or carbohydrates to keep their blood sugar levels stable is very important. Have a discussion at one of the team meetings to identify the support activities that team members can help with when they are too emotionally impacted to pro-vide direct intervention. Remember, everyone feels better when they can do something to help.

> **What if one of the teachers passed away at school and the other staff members were more upset than the students? Staff wanted formal acknowledgement but administration worries that this will esca-late the situation, so they don't really address. There was no staff meeting. Many staff were upset with the lack of response.**

There will be those situations when a staff member dies and students may not have significant reactions to that staff person's death. On the other hand students could have intense reactions based upon their relationship with that staff person. In this case, observe the responses of students and then deter-mine the number of team members that may be needed based on the number of students who are expressing their grief.

It is appropriate for staff to want to have some formal acknowledgement of their peer's death. If the administration does not provide some response, they run the risk of creating a great deal of distrust and loss of support from their staff. This acknowledgment does not have to take place over the PA sys-tem. It can take place at a staff meeting at the end of the day. The staff most impacted can be given the opportunity to meet with district crisis team mem-bers. A message via e-mail or other social media communication or a letter can be sent to every staff person and students' families. Some staff will want time to attend the funeral and memorial service. Some staff will want a few days off before going back into the classroom. These can be done without upsetting the entire student body.

> **What if the teacher of a class that had the student who died is not able to cope with the incident and decides to leave? How do you**

explain to students that they have also lost their teacher (not that the teacher died but that she or he will not be returning)?

Following the Oklahoma City bombing of the federal building, hurricanes Katrina and Rita, the Sandy Hook Elementary School shooting and so many other situations having a direct impact on schools, teachers have left those areas. This obviously can be difficult for students as well as for other staff. Team members should discuss and prepare what they will communicate to students in a nonjudgmental yet positive way. The response should include that everyone has the right to manage what has happened in ways they feel is best for them. If remaining was going to be difficult for some, it makes no sense for them to stay because they would be less effective as teachers and less helpful to their students. If needed, consult with how other schools have responded to the loss of staff following a major incident. This is one of those contingencies that can be planned for before it takes place.

What if you have a teacher who encountered a crisis such as a death in their family during the day?

Any teacher who encounters a crisis in their family during the day needs to attend to that crisis. As this will be a sudden departure from the classroom, students will need an explanation. If what has happened is known and takes place in the morning, it is best to inform the students as they will likely find out quickly. Crisis team members can meet with the class to answer their questions and provide support. Other students of this teacher should also be informed. Students should be updated if new information is forthcoming before they leave for the day. If this takes place in the afternoon, at least the students in that class will need some attention. The crisis team can meet at the end of the day to determine the next step. A Fan Out meeting can be called for the next morning before students arrive, if the situation is likely to impact a larger number of students and staff.

What if a staff or faculty member reveals information (details) about the crisis? For example, in a case of suicide, which the staff had been told and/or agreed not to share?

What if staff are contributing to rumors, providing too much information or making derogatory or sarcastic comments to students?

What if the staff members make it difficult for me to perform as a crisis team member?

A staff person who reveals information they have been told not to share needs to be held accountable. Unfortunately, there will be those staff people who do contribute to rumors, provide too many details or make derogatory, sarcastic comments to students about all that is happening. This too is an issue of accountability and should be attended to immediately.

Any staff member making it difficult for crisis team members to perform what they have been trained to do also needs to be held accountable.

Prior to a crisis happening, staff should clearly understand the expectations that administration has of them regarding their behavior, verbal communications and interactions with other staff and students during a crisis. They should understand that certain behaviors are not acceptable and they will be held accountable should these behaviors take place. It helps to include this in a training for all staff that identifies the types of behaviors that can be expected during a crisis, those behaviors of students that call for immediate attention from the crisis team, the types of responses the crisis team will provide, who the crisis team members are, the behaviors that are expected of all staff and those behaviors that are not acceptable because they tend only to intensify the situation. It is also essential to put all this in perspective by being trauma-informed and educated as to how the brain functions during stress and what neuroscience now supports to be the most helpful responses in a crisis.

What if after I arrive, I realize that the victim is my son's best friend?

If, as a team member, you discover that the victim is your son's best friend then it is important for you to excuse yourself from the team and attend to your son. The purpose of having a team is to have a sufficient number of members who are trained and able to back one another up in such situations.

What if a child is a runaway and the mother reported that her child is missing? However, the mother also works at your campus and she is confronting kids?

If a mother who works at your school is facing such a significant crisis and is engaging in unacceptable behavior, administrative intervention should be immediate. The behavior may be understandable given the situation that person has experienced, however, if her behaviors are also escalating others it needs to be contained.

What if, in an accident, the faculty causes the death of a student or a member of the student's family?

If a faculty member accidentally causes the death of another student, that faculty member will certainly have a variety of intense reactions that need attention. That staff person may need protection from the reactions of others. Certainly there will be legal issues that may prohibit a great deal of communication about what happened. In this situation it is very likely that the staff person will be put on leave.

This is a difficult situation for everyone involved. Even though this may have been an accidental death, the parents of the student will still be in a great deal of pain and may take legal action against the school as well as that staff member. I am remembering how in Parkersburg, Iowa, after the beloved coach Ed Thomas was killed, the community embraced the family whose son killed the coach. Not all communities would respond in the same way. Much of what will happen will often be based upon the community's response to this situation and what the media decides to report. There will need to be ongoing responses and strategies that are initiated based upon the community response as well as reported discoveries during the investigation.

The students who relate the most to this staff person, as well as his/her colleagues, will have a variety of reactions. This situation will likely necessitate an extensive crisis response to help all those who are impacted by what happened. The classmates, peers and friends of the student, the student's family and families of other students who now are asking questions about the school's leadership and safety of their children will need immediate responses. The majority of these responses and communications can be planned out well in advance of something like this happening.

What should go on when we walk into a classroom during a crisis?

Schools who conduct structured Fan Out meetings with all staff prior to students arriving at school, present staff with the various ways they can interact with students, a prepared statement they can communicate, and what will be happening during the day. They are also given a list of student behaviors that indicate the student needs to see the crisis team and how they are to make this happen. They will be given updated information related to what happened, informed that they are to attend a mandatory meeting at the end of the day evaluate what helped, what needs changing or what still needs to be done. (The issues to be addressed in a Fan Out Meeting can be found in the Appendix).

What if a critical incident happens during the day? How do we respond?

The immediate response is to get with the most exposed as quickly as possible. If this happens in the morning, district team members can be deployed to help with what will be a triage-like response. Texting will happen immediately so administration must also text staff and students immediately with information they have and to simply communicate that they are aware of the situation and mobilizing resources. The entire staff needs to be mandated to attend a staff meeting at the end of the day to evaluate and plan for the next day. (The objectives of this End of Day Staff Meeting can be found in the Appendix.) This needs to happen regardless of the time the incident happens. If the incident happens within one hour of student dismissal, it is advisable to make a brief statement as to what happened and to let students know that counselors will be available after dismissal if they wish to stay and the next morning when they arrive. They also need to hear that they will be notified of any schedule changes when they return to school the next morning. A meeting with all staff will be difficult to convene as many will not have time to adjust their schedules.

Staff must also be informed to report early the next morning for a standard Fan Out meeting in order to be updated and given direction as to how to proceed that day. A few of the issues discussed at this meeting were described in the answer to the previous question and are also available in the Appendix.

The crisis team must also convene at the end of the day to review what they were not prepared for and what might still be needed to manage those situations. They need to identify their priorities for the following day and mobilize any additional resources or support they determine will be needed.

Students

What if staff and students are texting about what happened before either receive a message from administration?

Students and staff will be texting immediately and throughout the day. It is equally important for the school to be updating information, support and reassurance via the same social media students and staff are using. (This was discussed in detail in Chapter One under "A Teacher's Murder.")

What if most students learn about the "facts and rumors" of a crisis through the use of social media (texts, instant messaging, Facebook) well before staff are aware and ahead of what the news is reporting? What if they are streaming into the office, cafeteria and hallways and are not arriving at class as a result?

In addition to what has already been suggested regarding the administration's responsibility to be using social media as quickly as the students and staff, this question suggests that first students need to be contained. It would be recommended that an announcement be made directing all students to return to their homerooms to await further direction/information/updates. Order and containment is critical to minimizing additional escalation. The response might be similar to issuing a "lock in." A "lockdown" is issued when potential danger is already in the building. A "lock in" is called for when potential danger has not yet entered the building and it is for the safety of all not to be leaving the building until the area is secured.

The concern with students being in other than their classrooms or designated areas is that they may leave the facility. This is generally an issue seen at the high school level rather than elementary level. Students who leave the building may be placing themselves at risk as well as raising liability issues for the school should any of those students be harmed following an unauthorized leave. This should be discussed in team meetings. Schools are responsible for the safety of their students. Containment of students is a critical and difficult issue that safety and security protocol should address.

What if the girlfriend and other friends of the student's killer also attend the school?

These students need attending to immediately. Their concerns need to be addressed. The ways they respond to threats from others must be covered. Many will feel intense guilt and shame. They will also experience fear regarding possible retaliation. Maintaining adult presence with these students while in school will be necessary to protect them from possible retaliation. Cultural issues can further intensify responses similar to the reactions toward Muslims following 9/11. Depending upon the school climate and culture this may become a serious problem or one that is managed by students in reasonable fashion. (This was discussed under the 9/11 and Virginia Tech stories.)

If the students who may retaliate can be identified, schedules should be examined so the two groups are being dismissed at different times. Obviously, all students must be made aware that retaliation is not acceptable. This is a potentially volatile situation. There is the option of bringing together the two groups of students for what might be referred to by some as "gang intervention." Consulting with a law enforcement gang specialist may be beneficial when the threat is felt to be real. This is actually a growing problem as violence among our youth is increasing. This definitely needs to be addressed by both safety protocol members and crisis team members.

Often teen suicide is result of boy/girlfriend breakup. How do we deal with the person initiating the breakup?

The most common questions students ask about suicide can be found in the Appendix. Crisis team members should be well trained to respond to potentially suicidal students, know their legal responsibilities regarding the duty to inform and refer and be aware of the protocols following a suicide. They should also be aware of contagion issues and strategies such as the classroom presentation and the limiting of published detail, which can help prevent contagion or "copycat" behaviors.

What if an elementary student commits suicide; are the younger students told the cause of the death?

Yes, because they will hear others refer to it as a suicide and want to know what that means. It is important to know how children developmentally understand death to appreciate what will be helpful in explaining what happened. All that has been said earlier about confirmation from the medical examiner's office also applies, as do the responses provided about parents not wanting information given to students.

What if a student takes his own life in school in plain sight of other students?

Students who witness another student take his life will need immediate attention. Do not assume all will be traumatized by what they witnessed. Some will; some will not. However, crisis intervention remains the first intervention response. If four or five days later some of the students are still struggling, they may benefit from group support for the most exposed. (This intervention can be found in the Appendix under Time Specific Interventions.) Only include in this group those who were direct witnesses. Those who may have been related to the victim will also need the same intervention if previous efforts to help have not been beneficial. They too will need to be in their own group. Also remember that some reactions may not surface until months later. It is never too late to provide intervention. The comments about intervention protocols mentioned earlier also apply.

Following is a listing of questions that all have the same answer.

What if multiple students are killed or seriously injured on a school field trip?

What if a former student dies?

What if there is a death of a student in a school with a multicultural setting? How do we deal with the various cultural beliefs, teachings and protocols for such events? How do we remain sensitive to all groups and their respective beliefs?

What if you have a student become violent because they are so emotionally upset?

What if students blame surviving family or friends of the deceased?

What if one student is sitting by herself saying nothing and says everything is okay when asked?

What if a student is uncontrollably crying and can't hear what we are saying?

What if a student is overreacting?

What if students are very angry about the incident—someone getting shot and killed?

With high school students do you let them curse and express their anger? Do you take them out of the classroom situation and deal with them individually? What if it is the majority of students?

What if a child is emotionally inconsolable, has a history of emotional and social difficulties in the past at school, and the school does not have a positive relationship with the parent as a result?

What if the students seem like they are okay but later have residual feelings and emotions?

These student reactions are best managed through the basic crisis intervention strategies of attending, acknowledging, comforting, being curious, making meaning, taking action, and assisting students with what they tell us will help them the most at that moment in time and in the days that follow. Basically those who have crisis intervention training will be able to best manage all of these possible reactions.

What if the students in crisis refuse to listen and comply with requests?

The response would be no different than when noncompliance is occurring when the school is not in the midst of a crisis. There is a reason for their noncompliance that they may not be able to clearly express. Their safety and the safety of those around them is always a priority. Once this has been established, it will be helpful if crisis team members can use this as an opportunity to connect with students, not to apply disciplinary action, but to help them discover alternative ways to manage or regulate their reactions and behaviors. Being trauma-informed and educated as to how the brain functions under extreme stress is essential to knowing how to help students regulate their reactions and behaviors.

What if the students don't respond to me because I'm a stranger and they only want to talk to the counselor whom they know?

Children expect the staff in their school to be the primary responders helping them. When district team members arrive, students may be reluctant to accept their help because they do not know them. It will help if staff members known to students accompany district team members as they provide intervention. Keep in mind that students will have varying needs. What may help some may not help others.

Inherent in the crisis intervention approach is identifying what those in crisis tell us will help them the most and then helping them with fulfilling this. Being with friends will help some, while being alone helps others. Some will want to talk, others will not. Some may want to be with family, while others will want to stay at school with friends. Remain flexible. Take the lead of students. When students are able to express what will help the most be ready to try several interventions until one of them helps.

What if students are refusing to go to the designated safe areas and are being verbally or physically aggressive, blaming others?

Protocol must be in place for managing students who are out of control or engaging in behaviors detrimental to others. If staff are not available to contain the student, the parents should be called to take their child home. Even in crisis students must be held accountable for their behaviors. Aggressive, assaultive behavior is not acceptable nor is threatening other students, being verbally abusive/derogatory or blaming those who may have been friends of the victims. These are often survival behaviors driven by fear and intensified by past experiences. They are not generally willful behaviors, but an effort to let us know that what we are doing is not helpful or making matters worse. This is why it is important for crisis team members to be also trauma-informed and educated as to ways to help students/victims regulate their reactions.

What if the deceased individual was not popular, not liked, a bully? No one seemed to care that this person died. Do you initiate and continue the process?

Some students are not popular or well liked. The response to their death may be contained to a small circle of friends. Interventions can be initiated with the group or with individual students. Even if their friend was not well liked or popular, they will expect the same responses from staff and the school related to his death. They will understand that not every student in the school cares, but they expect to have the same attention given to them as would be or have been given to friends of other students who have died. Family members will also need similar attention. Do not underestimate their needs. If the school has honored other students with memorial services, they will expect the same for their child.

Oftentimes, a survivor of a traumatic incident does not want to be in school. So, how do we support, react and act in these situations?

Some survivors may want to be with others, while some will do better with time away for themselves. Respecting what they believe will help the most should be supported. The classmates of those who remain out of school will need to hear that this is really no different than needing time at home after a serious injury. In this case, the injury is the form of the emotional pain this trauma caused for their classmate. It will be helpful to have classmates send cards or other "get well" messages to their classmate.

How do you reintegrate survivors back into the class/school environment?

This is an excellent question and a process that is not always managed well or even initiated. Not only do returning students need help but their classmates and teachers will need some guidance as well. (A reintegration process can be found in the Appendix.)

What if a group of students (football team, band, etc.) wish to wear black armbands as a whole to remember a deceased member of their group? They wish to wear them at all games, performances, etc.

Some students will want to engage in activities in remembrance of their friend. Wearing armbands, T-shirts and creating memorial sites are all very common. The issues regarding memorials were discussed in detail in Chapter One. The references cited in that discussion provide a number of suggestions and recommendations. In this situation where students are wearing T-shirts or want to wear armbands, it helps to educate them to the fact that those visual references can be almost too much to manage for some, because of the reactions they create for them. It is important to teach students that all students need to have the choice to express their reactions to what happened and to manage in ways that are best for them. It will help after several days to direct those students who need to visibly show their support to direct their behaviors towards ways that support the surviving family members. For example, each student could be asked to write something on T-shirts and then those T-shirts could be collected and presented to family members. For families, simply seeing the sheer number of students express what they liked about their son or daughter can bring tremendous comfort. This gift from students can be far more healing for students and family members than words alone.

Regarding armbands, some professional teams wear those armbands for a single game while others wear them for the complete season and remove them before the new season begins. School settings are far more complicated. What one group is allowed to do, all groups expect to be able to do. To wear for one sporting event following the death of that student is appropriate. After that one display of reverence, students' focus should be directed at what they can do to show their respect to the family of that student. These are always difficult decisions and will be partially influenced by the customs and culture of the community. Small communities will make choices that are not necessarily wise for larger communities to follow. (Reread the information on memorials presented in Chapter One. Also reread what Virginia Tech did to honor the lives of those who violently ended on their campus.)

Crisis Team Members

What if a crisis occurs and several members of the team are not available?

What if too few crisis response members have been called to help?

It is recommended that district teams be comprised of a minimum of 10 members. Ideally each school should have at least two members with the same training as the district team. When a school experiences a crisis, its two members can initiate a number of responses while waiting for district members to arrive to assist them. When district members arrive they take their direction from that school's team members. Should a school need additional help, trained members from other schools in the district can be called to assist. This is the best way, in most cases, to ensure that there are enough trained members to manage situations that call for additional help.

What if there is conflict on your team?

Team members will always experience differences as to what each believes is appropriate. However, sustained, unresolved conflict is detrimental to the overall efficiency and quality of the team's response. When this is the case, membership must change. In this regard the team should meet at least quarterly to review potential scenarios and related protocols, but to also develop trust and confidence in each other's abilities and willingness to follow protocols. This is difficult to achieve when the team is not meeting several times throughout the school year. Teams who do not meet on a regular basis are not teams but simply a group of people who come together in a crisis and do the best they can at the time. Proficiency will be compromised under these conditions. The risk of mismanagement will be much higher as well as the risk of liability.

What if I am in an environment and no one has organized the safe areas and identified priority students?

Safety of all is always the first priority. Following this the priority is meeting the needs of the most exposed. Leadership in a crisis is critical to efficient, expedient stabilization of those in that environment. If the people in that environment have been so impacted by what has happened or were not organized to begin with, it is important to offer your expertise to the administrator for approval of your involvement. Hopefully they will accept your help. If the administration is not open to your help, then support your colleagues as best you can and are comfortable doing in a nonsupportive environment.

What if the principal and counselor of the school are supposed to work together to manage the overall response, but there is a conflict of roles and the administrator shuts down the response mid-response?

The administrator of that environment determines what you are able to do. All you may be able to do is to first take care of yourself and then offer support to others in ways that do not conflict with the administrator's mandates. (Additional suggestions are presented under the upcoming Administrator *What if* questions.)

> **What if I feel helpless and I cannot help control the situation?**
> **What if members of the Crisis Team get "stuck" in their own emotional reactions?**
> **What if you have protocols in place and still are not prepared for certain situations?**

One can never be fully prepared for everything they may be exposed to in a crisis. The reason for having teams is to have enough members available so if several team members need to step back because of their reactions, others can take their place. This is another reason why all team members should have the opportunity as a team, once the crisis has been resolved or comes under control, to process with other team members all they were exposed to, their reactions, what they learned and what they determine they will need in the future to be better prepared. (An outline of this Crisis Team Review can be found in the Appendix.)

> **What if during the course of the response another crisis occurs? (Example: another person dies, more violence, etc.)**
> **What if there are consultants outside our local school system who are eager to be involved? How can they make the necessary contacts?**

The response to a crisis is difficult to predict. In addition, one crisis can lead to another. For these reasons it is best to know beforehand who is available to help if needed. Potential consultants outside of the district can be invited to one of your team meetings to discuss their role should you need additional assistance. We always encourage school districts to have some form of an agreement with surrounding district teams should their help be needed. The important issue is that they have the same level of training and are agreeable to their role should they be called. If called, the team members of that school in crisis need to direct and manage the invited crisis team members. Those requesting help will best know the needs of students and staff, who may be most at risk and who may need what intervention.

Incidents

> **How do you know how many team members may be needed to manage a crisis?**

Not all situations necessitate a full crisis team response. However, it is really about being prepared for whatever the student response might be because it is often unpredictable. When making the decision as to how many crisis team members may be needed, it is advisable to just multiply that number by two. It is far better to have more than enough adult presence in that environment should the response be larger than anticipated. If the response is not large, then members can return to their own facilities. If there are not enough members present initially, control can be quickly lost and reactions escalate rapidly. It can take days to recover and stabilize the student population once this happens. It is far more expedient to have too many rather than too few counselors available when students enter the facility.

> **What if children of a number of families are living in an apartment building and witness a shooting or suicide? How should the school respond?**

Be prepared to greet those students the next morning and direct them to an area where members can evaluate their reactions. They cannot be stopped from telling others, so be prepared for responses from others. This is not likely to need a full-scale response. Certainly the teachers of those children should be notified and team members available to answer questions they will likely have regarding how to interact with those students. The parents of those families should also be contacted to gather information and to extend the offer of help and provide information as to how to help their children.

> **What if a large-scale crisis occurs like 9/11?**

Large-scale incidents have been discussed throughout the text. It will help to return to the lessons learned from hurricanes Rita and Katrina, 9/11, Sandy Hook Elementary, Virginia Tech and the Texas wildfires.

> **What if you cannot communicate due to a language barrier or what is being suggested is in conflict with the different student cultures? What if the community/school setting is a Christian school, and this particular religion is judgmental about suicide, and a teacher, student or family member committed suicide? Do you insist on certain things when conducting crisis intervention?**

Having representation on the team for the diverse cultures of the student population is essential. Although these representatives may not be trained counselors they can certainly advise teams as to what responses are or are not appropriate for that student population. They can help calm and soothe students and when necessary translate what is being communicated. This also speaks to the one question about Christian schools and their beliefs about suicide. Ultimately culture and faith must be respected.

Is it appropriate to provide a spiritual component to the grief process when counseling students? Questions usually come up about "why" did this happen to me? How do we respond?

The faith-based needs of survivors certainly ought to be supported by the ministry in the community. It does help if you spend time with the ministers in your community or invite them to one of your team meetings to determine how they will respond so you can best decide whom you feel comfortable referring families to should they need the support. Schools are generally more comfortable referring students/families for assistance from clergy/ their communities rather than having this assistance provided in the school setting.

The question about why did this happen generally cannot be answered adequately. It is best in this case to redirect the question by focusing on the fact that we may never know why, but what is most important is how what has happened is affecting that person. How has it changed the way they now think? What worries has it induced? What reactions are they now struggling with as a result of what they experienced?

What if there are multiple deaths (many members of a family) and there are several members in various schools?

Standard protocol is for administrators to communicate with other school administrators when a situation like this happens. Each of those schools then initiates their crisis procedures.

What if we have a teacher who has had a health scare and has to be taken out of the building in an ambulance? What should be told to students, staff and parents?

If a staff person is taken out of school in an ambulance, a brief announcement should be made, as texting will begin immediately. Provide general information. Briefly let everyone know that as additional information is received it will be updated. Sending team members to that teacher's class may also be helpful. If the staff person holds a position other than as a teacher, sending counselors to those students that staff member spends time with, for example as a coach, will also be helpful.

> **What if the crisis erupts from an outside source that moves into the school: for example, angry neighborhood parents are upset over an issue dealing with their children; an argument and fight erupts in the office area. How should the crisis team handle the situation?**

When a crisis situation takes place outside the school itself but continues to escalate and be brought into the school, safety and security protocol must be initiated immediately. It would be expected that if someone from the school is aware of what is taking place outside the school, he or she would notify administration, who could then order a temporary "lock in" until that conflict is stabilized. ("Lock in" is discussed under the Parent *What if* questions.)

> **How do you deal with people who aren't directly involved with a situation, but kind of jump on the "bandwagon" and act like they are directly involved?**

When students or staff who are not associated with the victim or directly involved with what has happened act as if they are, they are basically telling us they need attention. Not giving them this attention will likely intensify their need and the behaviors they engage to let us know we need to respond to them. Teachers often mention this occurring with students. Whatever the need, whatever their relationship to the victim or whatever happened, they need our attention. In order to minimize further escalation or contagion, provide them the attention needed.

Timing

> **What happens if a student who is at home alone during a school day (has called in sick), but is threatening suicide to her friends/classmates through text messages, then stops texting and one of those friends comes to your door in a panic?**

Call 911. Call the parents at home and at their work place. Parents may be at home but unaware that their child is in the process of ending his or her life. Once the emergency is handled, thank the reporting student for being a true friend and telling an adult. However, also let this student know that the classmate threatening suicide may be angry at him or her for telling and you would hope he or she would allow you to help should this happen. Reiterate the courage it took to tell—that although that student may be mad with him or her, others understand that being a friend sometimes means doing something that may not be initially appreciated by some.

The following questions are answered in one response.

What if an attack occurred during the arrival or dismissal of school when "control mechanisms" are most vulnerable or least effective?
What if a crisis occurs during extracurricular activities and the crisis response members are not on school grounds?
What if the situation occurs in the process of arriving at school in the morning?
What if a situation occurs during a school event—for example, with a football player during a game (on a Friday night)?
What if something happens on an off-campus trip?
What if you have a crisis the last few days of school?

When a crisis takes place during the day a triage-like approach is needed. The primary effort is to reach as many of the most-exposed students and staff before the end of the school day. The next morning, following the staff Fan Out meeting, crisis team members will be prepared to initiate recovery protocol for other students who are having reactions. When a situation happens on a Friday evening it is helpful to make crisis team members available at the school on Saturday. If it happens during the summer or other school breaks, opening the school for students or families to access counselors is also helpful in preventing further escalation and minimizing the need for crisis intervention services when students and staff return to school.

When an incident occurs at a time when crisis team members are not at the school, reaching them immediately raises the issue of their responsibility to be available by phone, text messaging or other means. Although crises do not occur every week, and thankfully not every month, a discussion needs to include scheduling team members to be on call. When members are going to be out of town or are ill, this needs to be noted on the schedule. This process helps prevent delays in getting team members to the school facing a crisis as quickly as possible.

Administration

What if a person comes into the office and violently injures (incapacitates) all office personnel (secretaries and administrators) leaving no ability to initiate an immediate lockdown procedure?

This speaks to school safety and security rather than recovery interventions but it is frequently asked. Even today, after all that has happened, many schools maintain an open-door policy. Those entering are allowed to enter unescorted areas where many students gather. There remains a strong belief that "it won't happen here." Offices close to the school entry points should be equipped with panic buttons. Layout of those offices should be such that it becomes almost impossible to reach everyone before someone would be able to call for help.

Admission of adults into the building should involve standard procedures, such as having only one entrance available to visitors and visitors being required to have a scheduled appointment, not being allowed into the facility unescorted and not being allowed beyond the office area without a visitor's badge provided after signing in. The concept is to place as many deterrents as possible in the way of those intending to do harm, so that the number of possible victims can be minimized. Schools must simply do a much better job of securing their environments. No environment can be made 100% safe; however, the number of potential victims can be significantly minimized by consistently following basic safety protocols.

What if the administration does not see the importance in developing a crisis team?

When administration is not in support of crisis team response, little can be done. The primary reasons for this stance often is that administrators are misinformed about what crisis teams can do or not aware of the impact critical incidents can have on student and staff performance and behaviors. Over the years my experience shows that once administrators are provided basic information about grief and trauma's impact on learning and behavior and also attend a full-day training detailing the crisis team role, their responsibilities and the time-specific recovery interventions to be used, they are much more supportive of crisis teams and what they will be doing to stabilize the student population. They also better appreciate how this effort will help to minimize additional problems that can arise when crises are not responded to appropriately. Given the more recent incidents in Newtown, Connecticut; Chardon, Ohio; and other schools, there is a growing support for being prepared.

> **What if our administration chooses not to reach the entire student body/parents in hopes of diffusing (suppressing) the situation—in other words, not follow protocol, in hopes that further emotion/ anxiety is not elevated?**

When administrators do not follow protocol the outcome is usually a negative one. This was discussed in Chapter One, as well as what happened when administrators did not follow protocol related to communication with staff and did not conduct an appropriate "Fan Out Meeting" nor a staff meeting at the end of the day. When these types of protocols do not take place a great deal of mistrust and conflict between staff and administration results. It is hard for some administrators to grasp that when bad things happen in the lives of students and staff, they expect support and attention from the adults in their world or, in this case, from the administrators in their world. When this is not forthcoming students disconnect from adults, staff disconnect from administrators. Respect and trust are compromised. There are no positive outcomes.

> **What if we feel like a public school announcement is NOT appropriate? Kids/families NOT involved don't need to necessarily know because: (1) there may be kids in whom this info sparks emotion that doesn't need to be tapped; (2) kids may think the "copycat" thing seems/sounds interesting; (3) the entire school does not need to know and possibly get in an uproar—when only certain kids and families may need mediation; and (4) often—parents make things worse!—let them find out on their own—because they will—and they can talk amongst themselves—as they do!**

In today's world of social media the entire student body knows what is happening immediately. The entire school will know in some situations before administration. Not to at least communicate awareness of what has happened leads to mistrust and will actually increase other negative responses. It is far better to be proactive in the situation than to be reactive as it puts the school in a defensive rather than offensive position. The risk of contagion is related to the amount of details that are communicated, the popularity of the student involved and the risk of other students related to the attention that is given the student who died. Schools cannot prevent what the media decides to communicate. Contagion is directly related to media detail. What administration can do is help prevent contagion by responding immediately to students and staff in a proactive manner.

What if administration requires you to do something that you are very uncomfortable doing?

Be quite clear about being uneasy. Indicate that you want to help, but you are concerned that you may inadvertently place the school and the administrator at risk because you are not trained to do what is being asked. If the administrator insists that you comply with the request, you may want to consult with your union/teacher representative. It is advisable to have a written record of the situation and what you specifically did not agree with at the time. Do make sure that one or two in authority are aware of this conflict. Obviously, your purpose is not to increase the conflict, but to respond appropriately to those in need and within your skill level and role. You should certainly be aware of and follow the code of ethics and conduct of your professional licensing association.

Appendix

Summary of Lessons Learned

Standing alone without the power of and the details within the stories that produced these lessons somewhat diminishes the significant role they play in healing, recovery and preparing you, as a responder, for all you will be faced with in the midst of assisting others. You are encouraged to read the stories that shaped these lessons so as to best appreciate their value in helping you best manage the sometimes hidden, subtle and multi-level impact they have on everyone directly and indirectly exposed to traumatic incidents.

Chapter One: Past Tragedies

Oklahoma City

The effects of a traumatic incident are rarely contained to its direct victims.

It is crucial that schools and community mental health agencies, behavioral health care service agencies, child and family services come together to form a trauma-informed community task force. The goal is to provide a coordinated trauma-informed safety net of services for all who are impacted by traumatic incidents. This includes schools because this is where children are most accessible for help.

There remains a continual need for trauma education and training in spite of the large-scale efforts since 2005 by the National Center for Trauma Informed Care (2011) to increase awareness and to assist community schools and agencies to not only become trauma-informed but to trained in various trauma-based practices.

The facts of what take place in the midst of and following traumatic situations are rarely remembered as easily and as intensely as the memories, sensation and emotions triggered by one iconic image.

Physical reminders of a traumatic event can sustain and prolong unwanted reactions and memories.

Memorials do allow people to come together to support one another, as well as express their feelings in a supportive environment. Still, research shows that for some those same memorials remain a painful memory. The question remains, "Do permanent memorials belong in our schools?"

Given what we know about trauma today and the experiences of others in the past, schools might wish to consider supporting the creation of a memorial in the community. Those who find comfort in visiting can do so, while those who are uncomfortable also have the opportunity to avoid the memory.

Prior to attending to the varied needs of students and their many possible reactions, crisis team members need to quickly review all the possible reactions and interventions that may be necessary. In doing so, they will be better prepared and less vulnerable to being overwhelmed by student and staff needs. This information should be part of any recovery protocol manual.

When interventions in a crisis situation are not producing the desired outcomes, we as helpers are vulnerable to compassion fatigue. It is critical that possible alternative interventions be easily available when initial responses fail. Equally important are self-care interventions to help prevent compassion fatigue.

Hurricanes Katrina and Rita

It makes sense in today's world that schools have emergency contingency plans prepared ahead of time. All communities are more at risk for experiencing the large impact of trauma-inducing catastrophic events.

It is very important to identify the expectations that primary responders/ crisis team members have about what they hope to accomplish and how they anticipate others will respond to their efforts to help. When expectations are not in line with reality due to the varied ways people react, responders become more vulnerable to compassion fatigue and in some cases vicarious trauma.

Professionals are just as vulnerable to the effects of traumatic exposure as are nonprofessionals. Self-care is a critical issue often overlooked among professionals. As indicated earlier, interventions related to self-care need to be an integral part of the recovery process.

The Houston story also points out that one crisis can be followed by another crisis. Contingency plans need to be in place. Additional help from crisis teams outside the school district are crucial in the event of multiple crises, especially one too large for the district to manage alone.

Exposure and its stressful effects will remain as long as what people have been accustomed to in their communities is no longer functioning or available as a result of a traumatic event.

One of the important questions to ask when briefing primary responders after their work is completed is, "In the midst of a crisis there is always something or someone that brings a smile to our face or helps us reconnect to our strength and resources. Who or what might that be for you?" When responders are unable to provide personal examples, it may be an indication of compassion fatigue.

In the midst of crisis people will do best when they are actively engaged in doing something. It is in the doing that people in crisis begin to heal.

Professionals frequently do not realize or are reluctant to acknowledge, or get help for their personal reactions. This only prolongs those reactions, leaving them far more vulnerable to compassion fatigue and vicarious trauma.

A Teacher's Murder

In today's world of immediate connections via social media, it is critical in a crisis that school administrators immediately connect with their staff and students via the same social media they use. Failure to initiate immediate communication will leave staff questioning administration's level of preparedness and competency to manage what has happened. Although it may not be true, it can also leave staff members feeling unimportant and that their concerns and feelings do not matter.

Understanding the needs of staff is essential to empowering them to engage in practices throughout the day that are supportive of students and the overall efforts to restore calm throughout the facility. There are critical issues that need to be immediately addressed and communicated to all staff at one time in a way that is supportive, sensitive to their needs personally and professionally. It should afford them the opportunity to express their concerns, clarify their roles and responsibilities.

Instilling a sense of safety in students and staff goes beyond the physical presence of resource officers.

A sense of safety is supported and instilled when adults caring for at-risk students (any at-risk individual) have some information as to what may work and what will likely make matters worse. This is especially important during a school crisis, as at-risk students may need additional attention.

The reactions of staff must be acknowledged and normalized. Directives as to ways they can care for themselves are also needed to help them regulate their reactions. They must feel empowered by being given the opportunity to verbalize their concerns, ask questions and make suggestions.

The one question about what to say to kids during a lockdown stresses the importance of training in this area.

In today's world of instant messaging, all staff should be reminded and given time, once all are safe, to call or text family members to let them know they are safe and will be home after making sure that their students' needs are met.

The Killing of a Beloved Coach

This experience focuses on the parents of the students whose children were witnesses to the murder of their beloved coach. It reminds us that just as professionals are vulnerable to compassion fatigue and vicarious trauma, so too are parents.

From a trauma-informed perspective, this issue is the very reason that communities are urged to initiate a trauma-informed task force consisting of the major mental health facilities, child and family care providers in the communities whose staff are committed to working interactively with schools where children are most accessible. In such a network all would have the same training so they are on the *same page* as to the needs of those who are in crisis or in trauma. This trauma-informed group of community professionals can then be called upon to work with students and their parents when school staff cannot do so directly.

The Unexpected

It was always my experience that some intervention was better than no intervention. However, for the intervention to be the most helpful, it had to be directed at helping those in crisis achieve some degree of stabilization (self-regulation) in their immediate lives. To achieve this, in ways those in crisis felt safe to engage, the intervention process needed to be explained and accepted by the participants. It also needed to be structured, its objectives supportive of stabilization efforts and adhered to by those providing the intervention.

It is always easier to send elementary staff to assist at the high school level, where cognitive approaches are more developmentally appropriate, than to send high school staff to assist elementary-aged children where sensory based, nontalking interventions are more appropriate.

For a group intervention to be safe and beneficial for those in crisis, it is critical that the expectations of the intervention are clearly presented, that it has achievable appropriate objectives, which are guided by specifically structured questions that allow participants to reveal their many varied thoughts and reactions in a safe manner. In addition, those leading such an intervention must be prepared for the unexpected and be prepared to remind participants of the choices they have available to them if whatever is happening does not feel safe for them.

Safely Helping Those in Crisis

There is a time when some individuals do need help exploring and processing their emotional reactions. If one understands the needs of those in crisis, doing so when in crisis and in a group setting with peers is not the time. What they need most is to discover that what they are experiencing is not unusual, that they can regulate those reactions even for short periods of time, that listening to others can be extremely helpful in discovering that they are not alone with their reactions and that appreciating each other as survivors brings a sense of comfort and hope. It was these two experiences that led me to developing a process that was not mandatory and would not allow for the processing of feelings.

Wildfire: An Unexpected Delay in Recovery

Given the changing ecological conditions of our planet, weather patterns are likely to bring greater disasters. Contingency planning with neighboring school districts and counties that may be required to absorb large numbers of students, as was the case in Houston, is especially critical. Contingency disaster planning is critical to minimizing extended trauma. In this case, mental health needs were great but even greater was providing and sustaining resources for meeting basic needs. In many ways, the entire community had to rebuild their lives all over.

When Organizations Are Not Trauma-Informed

First responders are vulnerable to vicarious trauma. Unfortunately, the care needed by first responders is often forgotten or not attended to because of limited resources to assist them, or because they get lost in the demands of work that has gone unattended because of the crisis.

Crisis Team/Responder Issues

In crisis situations what we say and what we ask are critical to effectively helping survivors stabilize, manage, and discover their inner strength and resilience. As crisis team members, we ought to be proficient in providing crisis intervention and know all the possibilities of how we might respond and act before entering that crisis. This can be prepared far in advance of crises happening.

Legal counsel should review all protocol for possible vulnerability to litigation. Once approved, one of the responsibilities of a crisis team member is to monitor team responses to ensure they are following protocol, especially when members from other teams are asked to assist.

Be prepared with immediate accessibility to valuable resources and prepare yourself before entering that crisis.

District-wide teams who do not come together at least once a year to share all they have experienced are not learning to be better prepared, more effective and efficient in their responses. When these teachable moments are lost, the valuable lessons they teach are lost.

Survivors of Suicide

These are the voices of nonfatal suicide attempters and their thoughts. They indicated these thoughts repeatedly occupied their lives prior to their attempts. They reflect reality, but also distortions about themselves, others and the future. They also reflect attachment issues with parents.

Using positive verbal responses to reframe their thoughts not only frequently failed but, at times, led to a long list of negative, "yes, but" replies. This is when I realized that their thoughts were likely shaped by their experiences at home, which would be impossible to change in the short time we would be meeting. I believed the only way to move them to a different way of thinking was to involve them in experiences that resulted in strength-based, resilient focused thoughts about self, others and their future.

If we want children to be resilient, we need to engage them in experiences that induce strength-based thoughts about self, others and life. Trying to do this initially with suicidal youth using verbal efforts will be difficult.

Having knowledge of the thought processes that occupy the lives of potentially suicidal individuals provides the opportunity to connect with those individuals by acknowledging our awareness of the thoughts they are likely having or had at some point.

Listening and helping potentially suicidal youth focus on the fact they are not wanting to die, but instead wanting something or someone in their lives to change, can help to shift their thought process to more appropriate problem solving.

These thoughts of surviving siblings reflect the disrupted parental attachment that is frequently experienced by surviving siblings as well as the distancing from peers, who no longer know what to think about them or what to say. Such disengagement places surviving siblings at risk.

There is no absolute assurance when dealing with those who have already attempted that they will not attempt again.

Helping nonfatal attempters develop areas of competence to enhance their sense of worth and esteem is essential to their resilience in the face of crises they will continue to encounter in their young lives.

Keep in mind, it is the action we take to help them that matters the most in bringing about changes in the way they think about themselves and life.

Failure to meet with students following the suicide of another student is failure to take action. It is essentially ignoring their need for attention following an experience that can leave them with many questions and fears. The absence of this attention fuels their sense of alienation from the adult world and leaves them feeling that adults really do not care. Unfortunately, the vulnerable youth are also left to think, "I guess it's going to take a few more suicides before they decide to take us seriously." The logic makes sense to them and they will take action.

Survivors of Homicide

These statements reflect the intrusive memories, startle responses, fear, sense of hopelessness, revenge and a constantly terrifying readiness for trauma to happen again not only to others but also to themselves. They also tell us the body remembers the many sensations and sensory elements (sounds, sights, smells, touch) it was exposed to in traumatic situations. The reactions experienced can then be activated in the present when similar sensory elements associated with what happened occur in the present. This is why any intervention with traumatized students needs to include a variety of self-regulation activities that can be easily learned and used as needed. This is important for learning because as long as victims are activated or in the state of arousal, that intense anxiety makes it far more difficult to focus, retain, recall and make sense of what is being communicated.

Whatever children experience in trauma, adults can experience as well. This sister's response involved magical thinking, generally expressed by younger children. This teaches us that school staff are not immune to the reactions of their students following traumatic incidents. They too need attending in the same way we attend to children following trauma.

This mother's story indicates that, with a little help, those who suffer incredibly painful losses can discover their resilience and do for others what others have done for them.

This father demonstrated that, in his efforts to cope with his son's murder, he needed to do something. When surviving children and adults alike are not provided supportive, self-regulating opportunities to do something meaningful, this *need to do something* can take the form of more primal, sometimes dangerous survivor responses.

This mother's response embodies much of what has been described in previous experiences when both children and adults alike became vulnerable because trauma-informed intervention was not provided.

Multiple Deployments: The Worries of Children of Military Families

The children of military families must also be considered potential victims of war, even when away from the war zone.

What we learned was this one nonintrusive drawing activity brought us quickly and safely into the private world of these children in ways that simply would not be accomplished by the more intrusive approach of verbally questioning them about their worries. We learned that such insight is obtained quickly when using a medium children feel safe using.

The Gulf War

Drawing becomes a vehicle for communicating across diverse populations and transcends the limits of language. It allows children to use symbols accepted in their culture to depict the universal subjective experiences of trauma, in this case war—the terror, hurt and anger, revenge, accountability, feeling unsafe and powerless. In many cases the images used to depict their experiences are very similar regardless of cultural differences.

It was this one experience that convinced me to develop a more comprehensive intervention using drawing as the primary medium for addressing the universal subjective experiences of trauma. It taught me how many valuable lessons can be learned from survivors when we give them the opportunity to tell their story in their own way through the use of drawing.

Summary

The major lesson these experiences teach us is that ultimately no community is immune from terribly traumatic incidents. There is absolutely no reason not to be prepared.

Chapter Two: Survivors and Responders of September 11, 2001

New York

When trauma occurs, witnesses, even those who are not in harm's way, may need as much support as those directly victimized.

Crisis teams must always be prepared for a new crisis developing as a result of the turmoil and the efforts to control that turmoil. What is acceptable and not acceptable behavior must be clearly communicated. Administrators must be ready to respond.

When those in a leadership role are not prepared to make major decisions during a crisis, it creates additional anxiety for them and can place those in crisis at greater risk.

Access to *backup* not only applies to staff, but to communication systems.

Identify beforehand those staff willing to stay behind if necessary to assist students with special needs. Also in a time of crisis, prior relationships do matter.

Plan ahead for those crises when the physical safety of students is threatened and parents are asking to take their child and their child's friends with them. Determine the information you need to record and how the parents of those other children will be contacted.

We learned that we needed to add a column to the parent's release form that indicated where that parent was planning to take their child.

Several staff on every crisis team need to have good experience and comfort levels when working with upset adults (staff included) when the building is in crisis.

It is recommended when dealing with agitated adults, especially those whom you do not know, that a male and female crisis team member meet with that adult to help them de-escalate. In addition, it is better for two team members to agree on the best action in a crisis than for one person to carry all that responsibility alone.

"We learned that involving parents in the decision to reopen a school was essential to their feeling safer about letting their children go back to that school. We found the schools that had greater parent involvement before 9/11 were able to reopen sooner than those who had less parent involvement before the events of 9/11. The majority of students returned to the schools where parents were more involved."

Engaging in behaviors that demonstrate support for parent concerns is far more powerful and beneficial than trying to use reason and verbal reassurance.

Just as children in crisis need choices, adults need choices as well to feel safe and be able to best manage while in crisis.

This is a story that is likely to be repeated many times over in the coming years. Being prepared ahead of time is the easy part. The hard part is not to hold on to the false belief that such a situation will never happen. This belief erodes preparedness and places all at greater risk.

Having help readily available for staff far beyond the initial crisis period of four to six weeks must be part of the planned crisis response.

Be prepared for staff turnover following a major crisis. It happened in New York and it happened in Connecticut following the terror at Sandy Hook Elementary. Also seasoned substitutes will generally function best in the aftermath of a crisis. However, all substitutes on a school's roster should be provided the same training as staff related to responsibilities during a crisis and the possible reactions experienced by students as well as themselves.

In this case, counselors were dealing with aspects of those missing in action and issues of anticipatory grief. There are many resources (see Appendix) that can help shape how children are approached under these conditions. This resource should be part of a crisis manual. Despite how a parent may suddenly die—or for that matter a student—that child and those student's peers expect the adults left in their lives (teachers/counselors) to say something. What is conveyed will differ based upon the cause of death, such as suicide versus homicide. It is important to know the many alternative ways to discuss possible death and death itself and to have these available as scripts in the crisis plan. In some cases, especially with younger children reading a book related to the loss of a parent/sibling/peer can be more helpful than anything we might have to say at the time.

When children are in a state of terror they are operating primarily from their midbrain, where reason and logic do not exist. When operating primarily from the midbrain/survival brain much of what is said cannot be heard or comprehended. Therefore, it is critical to meet children where they are living at the time by engaging them in a variety of activities that are safe and allow them to express themselves in ways in which they may not have the words or language to do so.

Even for professionals, the reality of what has happened may take time to actively become real. The initial shock to our nervous systems can make first impressions and reactions misleading. If we do not have some direction, some sense of what we need to do, when the reality that "Nothing is fine" sets in, all we can do is what we do. What we do, may or may not help.

Without a well-structured crisis plan available as a quick resource for getting us back into our thinking brain and giving us very specific actions to initiate, what we do not do may also be very critical to the immediate and long-term well-being of everyone involved.

Collaborate. Know those professionals you might need to call for help before you are in a situation where you need them.

Ethnic issues aside, reaching out to those school families who may still be very frightened for the safety of their children, no matter the cause or reason, needs to be part of the crisis plan. When a principal—who carries tremendous authority—does this, it is as if he / she is speaking for the entire school. It means a great deal to parents.

We needed to be like pregnant women who have their bags packed. Schools need to have ready to go packets with student lists, parent releases, water, snacks, etc.

When you think it's over it's not. "The one-year anniversary was just a few weeks ago. Children were in school for four days before September 11. The news media was stirring things up with all its rebroadcasts of the news that day. We needed to spend time with both staff and students to normalize all their reactions and be available for those who found the anniversary more difficult to manage."

Schools need to be self-sufficient when it comes to a crisis. They need trained staff with assigned roles because the reality is help may not be available for some time.

If you are going to use identification badges, list on the back the critical protocol for staff to follow in an emergency.

We needed a buddy, to not be alone during a crisis and in the days that followed.

Prior relationships with our neighbors and businesses in our area do matter. Many of them left their businesses to help us with the students. They brought water, let us use their phones and just became another adult presence that helped children feel safer.

Safety plans need to have alternatives, especially around evacuation.

Competing agencies have *egos*. Those we found provided the most appropriate help were the ones we had prior relationships with and who understood our needs as well as their limitations.

People who sleep on couches get grouchy. In other words, we learned that we needed to do a better job at self-care.

The goodness of people around the world is amazing. However, we learned we needed to dedicate staff just to talk with and manage all the phone calls, letters and the stuff that was sent to us.

When you are stressed, you get really thirsty. Mashed potatoes do help.

A crisis challenges every assumption and detail of what we think we can manage.

At the time of crisis we are forced to do all the things we have (hopefully) talked about and have been trained to do, but never thought we would have to do.

A good leader knows he/she cannot do it alone.

Titles do not matter in a crisis; relationships and colleagues do.

Schools that are about collaboration and have good communications are the ones that can mobilize the quickest.

Two Years After: Pentagon Families

Many things can happen that keep the pain and the memories intense. It takes time to move through each day and to gradually discover that the days are getting a bit easier. It takes time to recover and to adjust to the new realities of life. It takes the support of others to help integrate the meaning of such an experience into our new life. If we wish to help our own communities in times of overwhelming loss, we must keep ourselves prepared and informed with best practices. What has been learned in past years still remains critical to our effective response today.

"Our longevity was due to groups forming by word of mouth from survivors who first attended and then reached out to others. It was also because we insisted on keeping the groups private so survivors knew we would not give any information about them to the media."

"We had one group of survivors that was a closed group once it reached 10 people. That group, which I led with a co-facilitator, remained ongoing for over three years and the members continue to be friends and supporters of each other all these years later."

Many of the survivors started coming four or five months after the attacks. They simply couldn't come before because of the life changes they had to manage in those first few months and because they were so traumatized.

Healing takes time.

Most literature focuses on immediate responses and ignores the challenges both survivors and responders face long after the media attention and outside help as left.

Self-care is not only essential for our long-term resilience, it is essential to the quality of care survivors expect us to provide over time.

Chapters Three and Four: Newtown, Connecticut

"Recovery is a marathon, not a race."

"I learned that when we are under stress we tend to breathe shallow rather than deep."

"Perhaps now" he told us, "people across the country will not fall victim to the false belief that it can't happen to them."

This supports what was mentioned in Chapter One about creating permanent memorials in schools. It also supports the importance of giving staff a voice, an opportunity to tell their stories. It also demonstrates that violence can precipitate more violence, in this case death threats.

Violence has a tendency to trigger more violence in many different ways, which needs to be addressed in crisis plans.

It is essential to everyone's well-being to know how to approach survivors shortly after a traumatic incident. In trauma every one is a survivor first, a professional second.

Litigation is always a concern especially in the midst of a crisis when so much is happening and when reason, logic and common sense are not always at their best.

We also need to exercise judgment and common sense and let young children know we are happy to see them and capable of giving them comfort especially when in crisis.

Always be prepared for the unexpected.

History does repeat itself.

Unfortunately, the all-too "It can't happen here" belief prevents people from even caring about the lessons that can be learned following any tragic situation.

"Culture is all about mission statements, posters, procedures and protocols. Climate is all about relationships and making those relationships strong and healthy by focusing on the positive we all have to offer."

This speaks to the recommendation in Chapter One about establishing countywide trauma-informed task groups to create a safety net of services for the wide range of people that can be devastated by traumatic incident. Establishing and sustaining relationships prior to a crisis matters immensely in a crisis.

... *synchronicity*, meaning that connections are important and things happen for a reason.

Although not directly stated, openness gives others the permission to be open, and being open can relieve stress and generate support. In addition, openness by leaders shows others that it is not necessary to hide everything in order to be an effective leader.

In the midst of one crisis, we can anticipate other crises. It really dictates that school systems provide numerous resources for staff to help them engage regularly in self-care.

Although not found in most plans, there ought to be in every crisis plan a plan that details the resources that are to be made available to staff along with activities in their schools that provide support, comfort and help in regulating their reactions for many months afterward.

"I run it over and over, which I know is a problem for me and I'm working on it. However, I still think I should have been there to pull her out of trouble, because I would have been out the door before her."

It is going to take time to discover which pieces fit with what other pieces.

This supports that there is no one intervention that fits every situation or every individual in crisis. In crisis we need to take the position of not knowing what is best for each individual. We need to remain curious so as to be able to identify the varying needs of those in crisis and what will matter most to each at that point in time.

"We now listen with a very deep, refined filter always searching for what might not be spoken in words, but what the heart might be expressing in actions or inactions. The filter is always there, but now it's more like a coffee filter instead of a colander. It's a lot more refined."

"Being prepared for a crisis," she said, "also means having a plan and ensuring that everyone who is involved in that plan is aware of the protocol, is practicing those protocols and has good communication and input into that plan . . . to hope for the best, plan for the worst."

In planning for the worst, we can arrive at a more realistic understanding of the many responses and strategies needed during and after a crisis by examining possible scenarios and introducing a long list of questions beginning with "What if . . . ?"

However, even the most comprehensive manual is of no use if you do not have access to it.

"We now have a comprehensive list. If we had that list beforehand, it would have saved a tremendous amount of time and energy and decreased the frustration of the parents we were trying to refer after the shooting."

Susan said she's had to remind staff many times of grief and trauma responses and not to assume that people are going to remember.

"It is very important," she said, "to monitor each other as the healing process continues."

"When we do kind acts for other people, it really increases our well-being and it decreases our stress."

A trauma-informed environment will promote the value of generosity and provide the opportunities for traumatized children to learn and feel the benefits of being generous.

"Starting every day and ending every day with exactly what you're grateful for because that's where your focus will be brought back to every time you need support."

But again, when we are under a good deal of stress, we sometimes need to be reminded to choose those things that have brought us relief in the past.

If we are not engaged in good self-care as a weekly routine, we are not likely to immediately engage self-care actions when under stress.

It helps, in intense crisis situations involving many victims, when schools can integrate self-care activities into the daily schedules and the community can support victims by offering a variety of activities.

Be thankful for gifts large and small.

The thousands of gifts sent did create a challenge when it came to storage and paying for that storage, but they conveyed and accomplished what words alone could not.

Over the last 25 years research shows the physical and mental health benefits of living with a pet. Pets help lower blood pressure, lessen anxiety and boost our immunity (Davis, 2013). We also know that therapy dogs affect the release of various neurotransmitters in the brain. A pet also increases the production of oxytocin, which is heavily linked with bonding, while lowering cortisol levels associated with stress (Therapy Dog, 2013).

It is the creative process that matters, not necessarily the shape or form of what we might create. Creating is a process of discovering. As we discover whatever emerges, we are empowered. Being empowered makes it a bit easier to manage our fears and anxieties.

Laughter is a great therapy.

Sometimes wisdom comes from the youngest of children.

Chapter Five: Chardon, Ohio

What emerges is the importance of taking time to discuss the options with those who must return to the site of that tragedy on a daily basis. These are the individuals who matter the most. Although not everyone will be satisfied by the final decisions, their input is critical to identifying the possible solutions and arriving at an informed decision the majority can accept.

Biofeedback studies show that drumming along with our own heart-beat alters brain wave patterns. It soothes, calms, regulates and allows for self-expression without words (Payne, 2014). Drumming the sound of what they may not have the words to express or are afraid to express verbally, especially in a group setting, accomplishes this. It also induces harmony among its participants, which in this case was essential for all the participants.

This activity teaches us far more than asking participants directly about their safety concerns. The activity was structured in a way to allow participants to think about how best to use the resources they were provided, including one another. It also helped to display the extent of their need for safety (lie detectors, underground Navy Seal Base, etc.). It demonstrated the many methods and, for some, the limited methods they chose to protect themselves. It also clearly communicated what mattered most to them at this point in time.

The subjective ways children experience their lives are dramatically communicated not through language and not always through behaviors, but by engaging them in activities that are structured to reveal the ways they now see and experience themselves and their world as a result of their exposure to trauma.

The research is quite clear that those who do better than others exposed to the same tragic situation have a significant connection or attachment with a significant adult in their lives (Steele & Malchiodi, 2013). For these children the focus on connection must become the focus of intervention. It is critical to their resilience at school and at home in everyday life, which will certainly present them with additional crises.

Having a sense of safety is also about feeling connected, trusting those in their environment and having open communication about their concerns.

What they created had a unique meaning for each. What they were learning was that their shattered lives can be transformed. Safely discharging powerful emotions and being actively involved in re-creating the personal and meaningful memory of their friends and loved ones gave them a sense of strength to move forward.

Guided imagery, meditation, yoga and many other mindfulness activities are known to help reduce physiological and psychological reactions to difficult times, as well as to regulate reactions to stressful situations. They can be very empowering. Regulation is important because it is the core of resilience and the management of the intense reactions induced by trauma.

Not having a crisis team and a structured recovery plan in place created a number of challenges that could have been prevented.

Having prior experiences with or knowledge of those who are asked to help is critical to avoiding additional crises that can arise when relying on those who are not known to the team. This is critical for maintaining safety standards and quality of care.

Giving people multiple options to do what they feel is most helpful for them is essential.

Appreciating that in-school violence is traumatic for some but not for everyone is essential.

Understanding how violence can shatter one's sense of safety is as essential as providing those who struggle the most with safety the opportunity to find ways to manage their reactions.

When events in school happen prior to summer break, there are those who will be concerned with returning to school and families who will be equally concerned about allowing their children to return to that environment.

Involving everyone with multiple opportunities to discuss what they believe can be most helpful is essential to building a compassionate community and arriving at solutions that are supported by the majority of those most impacted by that incident.

Finally, when working with those who are the most exposed and who continue to have reactions and concerns in the months that follow, engaging them in structured activities that have multiple purposes is far more beneficial and healing than direct verbal interventions.

Chapter Six: Virginia Polytechnic Institute and State University (Virginia Tech)

In this day of social media, those in charge can quickly present a response that is prepared well before crises occur. That response can be crafted to keep the focus on what is being done to move forward, on the strength and resilience of those involved and the values they work hard to uphold. Such a quick response can help combat the negativity, accusations and blame that may come from other sources.

It is critical to know beforehand what the city, county and state law enforcement departments are able to do to help manage the media. Keep in mind that in some cases there may be dual departments involved. This can be planned well in advance. Do keep in mind that, because of staff changes and possible changes in procedures, it is critical to meet at least once a year with law enforcement to review the extent of their help in a crisis.

The extent of the resources provided to students, families and staff at a time of crisis is obviously important. As insurance becomes more of an issue in this country, establishing the extent of services in a crisis that providers are willing to support at no cost becomes important to the well-being of the entire immediate community.

"If you want to stay here or go home, go where you get the best hugs."

School schedules are planned well in advance. From this perspective, critical periods in a schedule can be very easy to identify. Should a crisis occur during one of those periods, the specific resources or choices that might be needed can be planned for ahead of time. For example, 9/11 happened shortly after the beginning of school, in the midst of still adjusting to all the issues that emerge at the beginning of a school year. Virginia Tech happened near the end of the school term and close to graduation and the summer break for many. This created differently unique challenges.

The lesson we learn here is to listen, observe and respond to what matters most to those who are in crisis at that point in time. However, it's also important to keep in mind that what we might do one day may not be helpful on another day.

Having strong relationships with service providers who can also quickly mobilize multiple resources is critical to the well-being of all involved. This also addresses a question many schools ask as to what their response should be when crises happen during the summer months.

To plan appropriately, know beforehand the procedures related to the medical examiner authorizing confirmation of the victim by a loved one or family. Furthermore, being trained to assist with death notification, or at least to be aware of the process and what is communicated to loved ones and families ought to be part of crisis team member training. Using this information, team members can identify what role they might play to further support families at the time of notification.

It is very important that leadership in a crisis be previously identified. Equally important is that the leadership is driven by very clear objectives.

We've repeated many times over how important relationships are to recovery. This is no different regarding the training of crisis team members in the district.

We certainly do not want to make the assumption that, just because a number of people have been exposed to the same trauma, that they all need the same help. We want to have time-specific interventions that begin with the least intrusive and only move to more intensive interventions when survivors display, by their behaviors and reactions, they are in need of more intense interventions.

In reality how many schools actually have a motto that exemplifies their overall purpose? In reality how many schools look to their values as critical to driving the recovery process? In many cases staff when asked cannot identify their values. It was Virginia Tech's motto and values that strengthened and hastened their recovery.

The recovery process of Virginia Tech, driven by its focus on community, its values and motto, not only accelerated recovery but protected its staff, students and families from secondary wounding and prolonged pain. Furthermore, it allowed them to define to the world who they were as a community and a university, rather than allowing others, like the media, to define them.

Similar to the listing on campus of those who died in the war and earned the Medal of Honor, and the pylons inscribed with their values, this memorial became another symbol of their relentless spirit, their courage to move forward and their determination to never forget.

They had so many volunteers they had to make the shifts 15 minutes, so everyone who volunteered was able to serve as an honor guard.

Giving people opportunities to do something in a crisis is empowering. It gave them a sense of empowerment, a voice in their community. It also allowed them to know that there is no one right way to think or feel although many do experience similar thoughts and feelings.

"When you let students do what they need to do, they find artful ways to take care one another."

We never know what kind of connections or relationships may be the most helpful. Listening for connections that may be significant for each survivor and trying to support the facilitation of that connection can be as healing has any formal intervention process.

You need to be sure to take care of yourselves, to remain vital in this work, because you do make a difference in the lives of those individuals you meet.

Using a *What If . . . ?* Process for Training Teams

Following is an example of how thinking, in terms of *What if,* helps us to identify the many contingencies that teams can prepare for before crises happen. Participants worked in five separate groups to develop responses to the scenario presented. Groups were given 20 minutes to identify their responses. A new element is introduced into each scenario as it unfolds throughout the day. The new element will be in bold and reflects the responses and resources needed following the additional "What if . . .?" scenario. Once all groups identified their specific tasks, all participants came together to discuss and add to their individual group responses.

The purpose of this activity is to identify what responders know, do not know or have not thought about. The responses presented below are those of responders from several communities. The results were used to help teams identify their strengths, areas of weakness, the need to develop additional protocol or rewire existing protocol.

Group One

What if three students in a school of 1,200 students open fire? You are in the office and notified almost immediately. An Incident Command Center is rapidly established. It will be 10 minutes before police arrive. A number of students have already made it out of the building.

Who will make up your command center?

- *Principal: establish contact with superintendent*
- *Pre-establish code red team if possible*
  - *Code red team is nonteaching staff, administrators, etc.*
- *Whoever is in the front office becomes part of the command center*
- *Nonteaching staff: secretary*
- *Two key people should be ready to handle contact with outside resources and make immediate decisions*

What will be the tasks of each?

- *Prioritize communication—communicate lockdown, call 911 (land line)*
- *Gathering information:*
  - *Identify injured students*
  - *Where are perpetrators?*
  - *Think about key people in each zone of the building*
- *Don't rush to aid anyone (don't defy the lockdown)*
- *Must work with local police officers concerning policy*
- *One person in communication with police*
- *Communicate with school staff and school nurse*
- *Utilize color-coded cards in the "to go" kits to be used at the evacuation site*
- *Phones—send out consistent message. Use prepared scripts.*
- *Goal: to protect life*
- *Stop bells from ringing*
- *Get buses lined up in case of emergency. Plan for emergency drivers.*
- *Establish lockdown rules*
- *Have students turn off cell phones*
- *Educate students about plans and their roles in case of emergency*

Group Two

What if the police arrive and immediately contain the shooters? Unfortunately a number of students and staff have been killed. A number of students did make it out of the building despite the lockdown. Medical personnel arrive. Media is on the scene. Police order an evacuation.

Identify what needs to be done, who needs to do it, and what issues related to these tasks may need special attention.

- *Crisis team goes door to door to alert staff and students of evacuation*
- *Fire drill procedures*
- *Put parents to work that show up to help*
- *Map evacuation route "not past fallen (dead) kids"*
- *Special attention to special needs students*
- *Have student rosters at another site*
- *Sweep of the building*
- *Have a plan where to send parents*
- *Use media to get information out*

Group Three

What if shortly after students are evacuated, police discover a bomb and call for the bomb squad? As the bomb squad arrives, there are several severe explosions triggered by a fourth student. The facility will not be available for days, perhaps weeks. You still need to meet with students/parents and staff. A temporary location has been arranged to provide intervention.

Identify what behaviors you can expect from students/parents and staff. Also identify issues/concerns about the kinds of interventions to be provided and the resources needed to provide these interventions.

- *Student reactions:*
  - *Terror*
  - *Anxiety*
  - *Anger*
  - *Refusal to go back to school*
  - *Grief*
  - *Guilt*

- *Retaliation*
- *Happy that someone died*
- *Staff reactions:*
  - *The same as student reactions*
  - *More medical conditions*
  - *Fatigue, headaches, etc.*
  - *Guilt and blame towards administration*
  - *Early interventions focus on physical and emotional safety*
- *Reactions of parents:*
  - *Accountability*
  - *Anger*
  - *Fear*
  - *The question "why"*
- *Issues and concerns:*
  - *What to say to kids and parents*
  - *Debriefing*
  - *Rumor control*
  - *Staff must come to grip with their own emotions before handling the kids*
  - *Use counselors / crisis teams / church / mental health agency*
  - *Communication between staff and kids*
  - *Meetings with parents*
  - *Support parents*
    - *Give literature*
    - *Talk to counselors*
    - *Talk with law enforcement concerning safety*
    - *Give facts about what is being done, what happened, and what they can do*
  - *Keep same routine as much as possible*
  - *Utilize staff to help other staff*
- *Resources in the community for staff*
  - *Utilize banks, secretary of state, etc. (e.g., lost drivers licenses)*
  - *Some efforts need to be ongoing*

Group Four

What if you now learn the building will not be available for the remainder of the school year (seven months)? You will need to relocate your students and staff to another school and share that space with the students and staff of that facility.

What questions do you have about relocation to another school? What will be your major concerns? What agreements need to be reached and become part of a Memorandum of Agreement (MOU) with facility administrators?

- *Transportation needs*
- *Notification to parents, staff (time, schedules)*
- *Setting up space, movement of materials, purchasing supplies, budget needs*
- *Teaching assignments, space for incoming teachers*
- *Special needs students / accommodations*
- *Extra-curricular activities?*
- *Trauma intervention: students, parents, staff, community*
- *Union concerns (support staff, teachers)*
- *State mandated tests*
- *Graduation needs*
- *Student files and paperwork*
- *Arrival / dismissal time*
- *Parking issues*
- *Progress of old building*
- *Security for both schools*
- *Media information*
- *Lunch concerns*
- *Orientation for students*
- *Community forums*
- *Liability in new building / more students?*
- *Culture conflicts*
- *Videotape / document the move*
- *Multi-discipline team to include:*
  - *Administrator*
  - *Union*
  - *Teachers*
  - *Community*
  - *Students*

Group Five

What if your school has been identified as one of the schools to absorb the destroyed school's students and staff. Your group has been assigned to work out the details and arrangements.

Who should be part of your group?

- *Staff from both schools*
- *Parents*
- *Principals*
- *Maintenance*
- *Student government*
- *Social worker*
- *Local clergy*
- *Community mental health*
- *School nurses*
- *Crisis teams*

What will be some of the major issues you will need to anticipate?

- *Over crowding*
- *Identifying PTSD students / staff*
- *Copycat (fear it may happen again)*
- *Safety issues*
- *Split days or alternative start finish times*
- *Rescheduling extracurricular activities*
- *Rewriting students schedules*
- *Replacing dead or absent staff members*
- *Dealing with media*
- *Outside resources for debriefing*
- *Space for privacy/counseling*
- *Texts and supplies*
- *Continuity of subject/classes*
- *Lockers*
- *Transportation*
- *Immediate funding for additional supplies*
- *Student reactions and behavior issues*

What resources may be needed?

- *Staff training*
- *Facility space within the community*
- *Using media as communication resource*

As you reviewed these responses, you likely had additional questions or suggestions. This is one of the purposes of a "table top" activity. Introducing a new "What if . . . ?" every 10–15 minutes, better replicates all the situations that can be created by a crisis. Responses, not previously needed, may become essential as the situation unfolds over time. This process helps primary responders become better prepared for all the possibilities a crisis can induce.

Time-Specific Interventions Following Critical Incidents

(All models are described in full, with questions and resource materials in Steele, W. (2013). *Critical Considerations: TLC Recovery Interventions Following Traumatic Incidents.* Clinton Twp., MI, TLC Institute, www.starrtraining.org/tlc/resources.)

Crisis Intervention (Begin immediately and as needed thereafter)

Objectives

- To meet the basic needs of those in crisis
- To return survivors to their previous level of functioning (Stabilization)
- To help survivors discover their inner resources and strengths
- To help survivors cultivate a resilience against future crises

*(The TLC Model incorporates psychological first aid into a crisis intervention response.)

Process

In a time of crisis everyone has inner resources. We help victims discover their inner resources by, Making Contact, Making Meaning, Managing Emotions, Taking Action, Finding Resolve, Focusing On The Survivor. Following are examples specific to each of these categories. Crisis intervention can be conducted with individuals or in groups.

Adapted from "Crisis Intervention: Promoting Resilience and Resolution in Troubled Times" (Echterling, Presbury & McKee, 2005) and TLC's structured sensory interventions, "Working with Grieving and Traumatized

Children and Adolescents: Discovering What Matters Most Through Evidence-Based, Sensory Interventions" (Steele & Kuban, 2013).

Classroom Presentations (Initiated first two days)

Objectives

- To gather information related to students reactions, concerns and questions
- To provide factual information, minimize rumors, change misperceptions
- To normalize reactions
- To identify appropriate behavior
- To encourage students as to the help that is available if needed and how to access that help
- To inform students of schedule changes, upcoming related activities

Duration

Thirty to fifty minutes

Classroom Guidelines

After expressing that this (loss/incident) is difficult for everyone including staff and that everyone is coming together to pull through this difficult time, present the factual information available and ask if anyone has heard anything different. If information related to details is new to you simply let students know you will check this information out and get back to them. Proceed with normalizing the varied reactions they are likely having, ask if there are questions, inform them of the days schedule and then how to contact you should anyone wish to meet with you. This is not a time to process feelings. You may observe students who are having a difficult time. You can meet with these students after the presentation to further evaluate their needs.

We strongly recommend that a core group of staff be trained to assist team members in conducting classroom presentations so all students can be reached within the first two days. Immediate presentations help diffuse unwanted student responses.

This outline does not include the different reactions survivors may have following different types of incidents such as: suicide, murder, non-violent trauma, grief, etc. Each situation will dictate a change in reactions to be normalized. We recommend "After the Crisis: Traumatic Event Crisis Intervention Plan" (TECIP) (Carlton et al. 2011) and "Handbook of Interventions Following Suicide and Trauma in Schools" (Steele, 2005) for this information.

Defusing
(Initiated as early as the first day
and as needed thereafter)

Defusing is an intervention that limits cognitive processing of an incident and is more appropriate for younger children. Only two basic questions are asked of non-witnesses in defusing. They include, "What have you been told or heard about what happened" and "Since this happened what is your biggest worry?" The two questions asked with those who were witnesses are, "What do you remember most about what happened" and "What is your biggest worry now? The responses of children are normalized, rumors and exaggerations of details are clarified and the opportunity to ask questions is presented. Following this brief cognitive focus, children are engaged in sensory-based activities designed to alleviate anxiety and help them self-regulate their reactions. Defusing is also beneficial with adolescents when they simply do not want to talk about what happened yet need to find ways to regulate their reactions.

Defusing Objectives

- To identify what children believe happened and correct misinformation as needed
- To identify worries/anxieties the children may have to help determine additional intervention that may be needed
- To help children regulate the worrisome/anxious reactions they may be experiencing

Defusing Guidelines

1. Defusing can be initiated the very first day.
2. Working with younger children dictates we remain flexible in our interventions. Be prepared to present children with several defusing activities,

as some will be more enjoyable and meaningful than others. Also Defusing may be all that is needed for some while others may need additional crisis intervention.

3. Students fully expect the adults in their environment to be the individuals taking care of them. Whenever possible, staff familiar to the children should be present.

4. There will be students who need to be provided additional crisis intervention should this initial intervention not be helpful.

5. Defusing can be initiated anytime in the days and weeks that follow especially when reactions are delayed or triggered by reminders.

One type of sensory support that appears unrelated to the type of the event and can be very beneficial to the healing process as reported by children themselves comes from cuddly toys (Alisic, Boeije, Jongmans and Kleber, 2011). Cuddly toys and *blankies* were very comforting for many children following 9/11 and are now often given to children by police, fire departments and hospitals immediately following critical incidents. It is believed that these tangible, comforting resources bring support when parents and others are not available. These supports also come in the form of imaginary friends, which that teddy bear can become, but which may also be strictly the imaginary friends children create when tangible objects like teddy bears are not available (Taylor, 1999; Henry, 2011).

End of Day Review Questions

This process is included in our recovery interventions because it helps to meet the basic needs of staff, as they have been busy throughout the day meeting the needs of their students/clients. The time frame for this process is one hour.

Objectives

- To evaluate current status of staff and students/clients
- To share new information & clarify rumors
- To determine additional need for immediate resources and support
- To prepare staff for possible upcoming problems
- To help staff care for themselves
- To reinforce positive aspects emerging from this event

Participants

- All school staff.
- Agencies—due to issues common to most agencies we recommend meeting with line staff separate from administrators/ managers/supervisors. Smaller agencies and/or administrators who insist on total staff participation at the same session are the exception.

End of Day Crisis Team Review
(To be completed end of first day and as
needed throughout the week)

Objective

- To determine actions and resources needed for the following day

Duration

Thirty minutes to no more than one hour. This review follows the End of Day Staff Review.

Process

Keep in mind that it has been a very long day for team members. They need to get home and relax as much as other staff. This meeting should be kept as brief as possible. Information from the End of Day Staff Review will help to define some of the actions that may be needed for the following day. Team members need to also identify what will be most helpful for them the following day. Before closing the meeting, it is important to review exactly who will be doing what the following day. Member's nervous systems will be hyper-aroused. After being hyper-aroused all day the nervous system will not slow down on command. It takes time. We recommend that the Team Leader stress the importance of taking twice as much time as normal engaging in whatever activity they use to reduce their stress.

Crisis Intervention Support for the Most Exposed
(Not to be initiated until the fourth day)

It is not uncommon that the most exposed will have the most intense reaction that continue beyond the reactions experienced by those not directly exposed. Often the most exposed benefit from one additional structured group intervention.

Objectives

- To allow the most exposed to discover that they are not alone with their thoughts and reactions
- To normalize these thoughts and reactions
- To educate about additional reactions they may have in the days/weeks that follow
- To identify the kind of support and resources they feel may make life a little easier for them
- To learn ways to care for themselves over the next several days, weeks, months
- To provide referral resources should they wish to talk with someone in the future

Time Frame

Not to be initiated/offered until the fourth day after exposure so participants can better determine whether the initial support provided was helpful or they feel they could benefit from additional help because of the unique reactions, which can emerge for those directly exposed. The actual group should be completed within two hours.

Participation

Voluntary. Appropriate for adolescents and adults. Not everyone directly exposed needs additional assistance. Choice and safety is a trauma-informed priority. Those who were direct witnesses must be in their own group as some of their reactions will be somewhat different from those who were related to the victim.

Group Size

No more than eight participants at a time.

Process

This is a supportive educational process. Its purpose is not to process or explore feelings, nor to allow for the ventilation of feelings. To allow this to happen places the participants at risk of losing control, of revealing more about themselves than should be revealed in a group of peers and exposing other participants to an emotional intensity that may intensify and otherwise regulated emotional state. It is designed to meet the listed objectives safely without processing feelings.

Simply ask the questions, allow the participants to respond and then move to the next question without comment. As other participants hear what their colleagues have to say, they come to discover the commonality they all share as survivors. This is a strong source of healing.

Group Leaders

We recommend two group leaders, male and female so participants who may have gender issues can feel more comfortable than they might with same gender leaders. Both leaders can be involved in the closing portion of the group when they summarize what has been learned, normalize reactions and provide additional helpful information.

Final Crisis Team Review (To be completed within two weeks following the incident)

Objectives

- To identify procedural or systemic issues of the school / agency which positively or negatively impacted efforts to support staff, students or clients

- To identify the reactions participants have in common
- To evaluate the overall team performance and actions to be taken to improve preparedness.

Duration

One to two hours.

Participants

This model is designed for use with school crisis team members or agency staff who have been frontline responders. In school situations some may be members of the local school crisis team and others from the district-wide team who assisted local school members during their crisis.

Two Months Following Exposure

"Structured Sensory Interventions for Children, Adolescents and Parents" (SITCAP®)
(**To be initiated two months following the initial incident or any time in the future if reactions persist or emerge in the future.**)

Objective

- To ameliorate the reactions and symptoms of PTSD
- To help survivors discover the inner resilience to heal

Duration

One hour sessions, eight to ten sessions

Process

These are manualized evidence-based intervention programs for use in school and clinical settings. They support the core principles and practices of trauma-informed care inclusive of addressing the physiological needs (self-regulation) as well as psychological needs of trauma victims.

Research related to TLC's SITCAP® programs can be found at www.starrtraining.org/tlc. These interventions are registered as best practices on the California Evidence Based Clearinghouse and the Substance Abuse Mental Health Services Agency (SAMHSA)'s National Registry of Evidence Based Programs and Practices (NREPP). Documentation as to their trauma-informed approach, detailed descriptions of their core processes and numerous case examples of the process are presented in Steele & Kuban, (2013). *Working with Grieving and Traumatized Children and Adolescents: Discovering What Matters Most Through Evidence-Based, Sensory Interventions*. Hoboken, NJ: John Wiley and Sons.

Fan Out Meeting Agenda/Traumatic Event Briefing

(Reprinted from Steele, W. (2013). *Critical Considerations: TLC Recovery Interventions Following Traumatic Incidents*. Clinton Twp., MI, TLC Institute, 71–72, www.starrtraining.org/tlc/resources.)

The Fan Out meeting with staff to inform them of the incident and prepare them for student response needs to present the following messages.

1. Factual data related to death. Warning: If the method of death is questionable, students, parents, etc. are to be told only that the manner of death is still under investigation by the coroner's office.
2. Rumors about the incident are to be reported immediately to the Trauma Team (Identify a specific person).
3. This is a time when many students may discharge a residue of emotion, which has nothing to do with the deceased, but provides them with an acceptable vehicle for catharsis. Any concerns about student emotional stability and risk are to be directed to the team immediately for assessment.
4. How to "transport" upset students to the Trauma Team or how to bring the Team to the student(s) if necessary.
5. All media questions etc. are to be directed to the assigned Administrator such as the principal or superintendent.
6. Staff will be informed of any new information that is provided Administration.

7. Staff are expected to meet again after school to debrief what took place during the day.

8. Staff need to hear that no one can predict what kinds of reactions they may see in students, staff, or even themselves and that at the after school meeting possible reactions will be further addressed.

9. The announcement to be read or presented to students must be reviewed and teachers given some guidance as to responding to student reactions such as:

   - Students having a difficult time can be seen by the Trauma Team.
   - Students can be assured they will have an opportunity as a group to hear and talk more.
   - Let students ask questions; note those questions the teacher cannot answer so that they can be addressed in the classroom presentation or as new information becomes available.
   - It is okay for them, as teachers, to express their shock, sad-ness, tears, or difficulty with talking about the de-ceased and that they too are looking forward to the classroom presentation.

10. Staff need to be reassured that there is enough staff support available, i.e., substitute teachers, team members from other schools, etc. should the response demand additional support. It is advisable that one or two trained people be identified as available during the day for staff people to talk with about their own reactions and concerns if needed.

Traumatic Event Crisis Intervention Plan

Rapid Assessment Guide

(Published in Markowitz, M., Carlton, G., Haddow, J., & Steele, W. (2010). *After the Crisis: Traumatic Event Incident Planning.* Clinton Twp., MI, TLC Institute, 117–118, www.starrtraining.org/tlc/resources.)

Date: _____

Form Reporter/Role: _____   School: _____

Incident:

Please respond to the five questions listed below. The information generated will help your team to better determine what is required to effectively meet the needs of your students and staff.

1. How many people, and whom can we expect to be impacted (clarify potential intervention needs on attached sheet)?
2. How much disruption, and what kind, should be anticipated?
3. What additional information is required and how might it be obtained?
4. What resources are required for the initial response (record anticipated interventionist staffing requirements on attached sheet)?
    i.   Is this an incident our building TECIP Team can handle in house?
    ii. If not, how much outside support will be required?
5. How critical/traumatic is this incident (what is the Scale of Response)?

Traumatic Event Crisis Intervention Plan

Scale of Response

Level 1

Situation confined to an individual or small group.

Level 2

Class or grade level affected.

Level 3

Multiple grade levels and potentially entire building impacted.

Level 4

Multiple buildings and sizable portion of district impacted.

Level 5

Catastrophic incident with widespread and profound impact on entire school community.

Traumatic Event Crisis Intervention Plan

Student Re-Entry Plan

(Published in Markowitz, M., Carlton, G., Haddow, J., & Steele, W. (2010). *After the Crisis: Traumatic Event Incident Planning.* Clinton Twp., MI, TLC Institute, 89–92, www.starrtraining.org/tlc/resources.)

Consider the following best practice strategies and accommodations for a student who is returning to the school after a significant event. These are students who are considered "closest to the trauma."

Prior to Student Return: A Modified Classroom Discussion

The classroom(s), which the student in question attends, should consider having a brief discussion prior to re-entry. But what should be discussed? Here are some suggested talking points to present.

- Good morning class, I want to take a moment to talk about (name of student). As we discussed, (name of student) has (suffered a great loss / recently been through a very difficult time). I'm glad to report that (name of student) will be returning to class on _____ and I think we should take a moment to talk about some things we can do or not do to make his/her return to school as positive as possible.
- First and foremost, like any other day here at school we need to show respect for one another. In being respectful to _____, please don't bombard _____ with questions about what had happened. If he/she wants to talk about it that will be his/her choice to do so.
- Remind yourself what it means to be a friend to someone. How do you want to be treated by others? It's perfectly normal to want to be there for a friend in need. If you have the urge to tell _____ that you are sorry about what happened, that's ok. That's a nice gesture. It's ok to share with _____ that if he/she wants to talk that you'll be there for him/her.
- It's also ok if you don't know what to say to _____. When something like this happens, we may feel unsure of what the right words are to say to someone. Again, this is normal. To say nothing is ok too.

- Remember, our class is a safe place to be and we want nothing more than to have everyone here feel that they are safe and that they belong.
- The best thing you can do is to treat _____ with the respect he/she deserves just as you do.
- If you have questions, concerns or see someone treating another in a way you feel is inappropriate, let a staff member know so they can intervene/ help.

The Day the Student Returns: Morning of the Return

It is suggested that upon returning to the school, a brief meeting is held with the student (possibly accompanied by their guardian) to let the student be reassured that they are an important person in the school, that the school is a safe place to be, and that support is available to them should they feel the need.

Being mindful that the student has the right to choose how they cope with the event and their emotional reactions to the event, the school should share several options/accommodations for the student. Some students may not use any of the suggested accommodations because they don't want to feel like they are getting "special treatment." Nonetheless, the opportunity for the student to have such supports available is certainly recommended.

- Having several key people who the student has a rapport with be "on-call" that first week back should the student be in need of having to talk to someone.
- Having a location nearby the student's classroom where he/she can go to "regroup" either by his/herself or with a classmate of their choosing.
- Have the guardian on-call should emotional reactions be too overwhelming that first or second day back to school.
- Consider a modified schedule if the transition appears to be "too much too soon"—possible go to half days for the first week back if necessary.
- Provide added support in less structured settings (i.e. lunch room, recess). If this is not possible, make sure staff assigned to these areas are updated regarding the return of the student and to vigilant of any activity in these settings that may be hurtful to the student.

Mid-Day Update

It may be advisable to have an identified key person check in on the student to see how the day is progressing for them.

Does the student have any concerns or questions? Do they want to call their guardian just to let them know that how they are doing? Remind the student of the options discussed and ask if they felt the need to utilize any accommodations so far.

- If you feel that having a morning, mid-day and end of the day meeting is too overwhelming and unnecessary, don't have the meeting. It is important to use your judgment in determining the need.

End of Day

As the end of the day approaches, it may be advisable to have a final, albeit, brief update meeting to see how the day's return went from the perspective of the student. An activity to gauge how their day went is provided below.

Ask the student the following:

- "On a scale of 1–10; 1 being that the day was very overwhelming and very difficult; 10 being that the day was very positive, where would you rank how the day went?"

The response will help determine an action plan for subsequent days.

- A response of 4 or lower may mean that another meeting is warranted to determine what appropriate course of action should be taken.
- A response of 5 or greater may mean that the supports for the following day may remain in place.

Ask the student if they would be willing to have another meeting at the end of the next day to see if there has been any progress. Ask the student what measure might be taken to help them move up 1 or 2 numbers on that scale. Modify the day 2 plan accordingly based on the responses.

Questions Students Ask About Suicide

(Reprinted from Steele, W. (2005). *A Handbook of Interventions Following Suicide or Trauma in Schools.* Clinton Twp., MI, TLC Institute, 63–68, www.starrtraining.org/tlc/resources.)

I am frequently asked when to address the questions students have about suicide. The best time to address their questions is when they are asked. This means being prepared.

The classroom presentation following a suicide is a natural place to introduce the questions students generally want to ask but may be afraid to ask because of what others might think, or students may simply be overwhelmed. Even in my experience of conducting presentations on suicide when there has been no suicide in the school, students are still reluctant to ask questions in large groups or classroom settings.

For these reasons it is recommended that in your presentation you simply present the question and then answer it; followed by asking if anyone has a different way of looking at it or other experiences where they may have given a similar answer but it didn't help.

Questions can be introduced by saying:

> *"I know you probably have many questions but may not be comfortable asking, so let me ask the questions other students have asked me over the years. I'll tell you what I told them."*

The questions we recommend be asked and answered follow. Posing these questions and then answering them will also let the students know that you are someone they can come to privately if they need to—and they frequently will catch up with you.

What if my friend refuses to talk with someone and says if I tell anyone he's thinking of suicide, he'll kill himself for sure?

This is not an unusual response. It is a form of testing and can be interpreted as a question. The suicidal person will be unsure of anyone who wants to help. Some will be more unsure than others. This response is from a person who is not quick to trust because of previous hurts and betrayals by others of his confidence. Still, what this person is checking out about the friend who wants to help is how much they are willing to fight to save their life. If the friend agrees not to tell anyone, they will lose his respect.

What needs to be said to the potentially suicidal person in this situation? A good response to the threat is:

> *"Look, you let me know you were feeling suicidal. If you didn't want help, you would never have said anything to me, so I'm not going to let it go. Come on. Both of us will go see someone."*

This kind of response lets the person know how serious we are and how much we care. It brings them back in touch with that part that wants to live. In most cases they will agree to see someone after hearing this. If they still insist on not talking and take off, it is critical that someone who can get to that youngster be told immediately.

Kids need to know exactly who they can tell and in what situations. When in school, there are the teachers, counselors, etc. When out of school, there are their own parents, police, and the phone operator for the Suicide Prevention Center, etc. Make sure they know where to go for help immediately. Schools can work out an arrangement with a 24-hour prevention center so that when kids call and identify the school they attend, the center can, if necessary, notify an identified person in the school.

What do I do if I want to break up with a boyfriend but he'll kill himself if I do?

When this occurs, the suicidal person is often very angry but unable to direct the anger appropriately. He/she is also devastated by the "rejection." In most cases, the breakup brings to the surface feelings around a much earlier rejection by a parent that the suicidal person is unable to separate out emotionally from the current situation, or is not consciously aware that the tremendous hurt he/she feels now goes back to a time long before the girl/boyfriend.

The friend who is breaking up with this person who is doing the threatening will also experience a lot of anger for such a drastic retaliation as well as fear that it may actually happen. The tendency is to act on the anger and say something like, "Go ahead," or "That's your problem, not mine." Sometimes the person reacts to the fear and either becomes immobilized or gives in to promising not to tell.

About the only response in this situation is something like:

> *"I know you're really upset; so am I, but I can't keep going out with you. You make me really mad when you dump suicide on me, but you are also making it clear that you really are hurt, too. Both you and I need to go talk to someone. I don't want you to hurt yourself, but I can't lie to you and say I want to keep going out with you, either. If you don't go with me to talk this out with*

someone, I'll have to tell someone, because I'm still your friend and I don't want you to hurt yourself."

If they are still talking suicide after this, it is imperative that someone is told. It's helpful to let students know that if they do this much, they have done as much as they can possibly do. Stress the importance of telling someone, as this will help minimize the horrendous burden of guilt should the person kill him/herself. A promise to talk to someone is not enough in this situation. They must talk with someone immediately. Once contact is made with a professional, they can take over, and the responsibility of the friend has ended. They were honest and did all they could possibly do.

What do I do when no one believes me or does nothing if I tell them about a friend I think is thinking about suicide?

The only thing to do when an adult, whether they are parents or counselors, refuses to believe it is unnecessary to act immediately is to go to someone else.

What if the counselor my friend is seeing isn't helping?

Sometimes counselors and therapists are thought to be miracle workers, and clients are said to be resistant or at fault if they are not making progress. There is no therapist/counselor who can work well with everyone. Personality clashes happen; backgrounds get in the way, and some problems are simply outside of the therapist's skill and knowledge.

Yes, it is true that sometimes clients unknowingly sabotage counseling, but it is also true that even the best therapist is unable to help some people who would do better with another counselor.

If counseling doesn't seem to be helping, first let the counselor know. A good counselor will agree and suggest taking another direction for a period of time and if that doesn't help, recommend another counselor. A good counselor will also recognize the need for an immediate referral if it is felt that continuing a while longer will not be helpful. The counselor who does not do this, but quickly says the problem is with the client, is likely not to be the therapist to continue to see.

Remember, suicidal individuals often do not want to die, they just want the hurt to end.

I would feel dumb asking a friend if they are suicidal. What if they weren't? Won't they think I'm crazy?

Yes they may call you crazy, but not really think you're crazy. By asking, you are showing how much you care, how much you pay attention to them, and how much courage you have to risk being wrong rather that assume they can handle things.

What if someone wants to die because things are bad and aren't likely to change— shouldn't they have the right to die?

Ultimately, the person does make the final choice as to whether they will live or end their life. It is critical to remember, however, that the person who is certain that suicide is the only way usually does not tell anyone or leave clues. Those who leave clues or talk to you about ending their life are crying out for help. If the response to their cry is "That's your choice," it may be interpreted as a rejection, and as a decision on your part not to get involved because you think they are not worth saving. Remember, the suicidal person often does not want to die; they just want the hurt to end and know of no other way or have not had the experience of someone being there for them when they need it most.

How do I get my friend to talk when he/she says it doesn't help to talk?

Sometimes people find it difficult to talk because they are confused and don't know what they are thinking. Sometimes they are scared that they will say something to upset the listener. There may also be a fear that as they talk, they may not like what they hear themselves say.

Silence is a difficult situation to deal with because the silent person is in control. It leaves the listener feeling frustrated, angry, and anxious about what to say or do. It helps in this situation to let the person know their silence probably has protected them before from people who were insensitive, mean, critical, or made them feel what they had said was crazy, stupid, or not serious enough to get so uptight over. If you can let the person know you understand this and that you're not one of these people and ask them who hurt them so badly that they feel like suicide, they are likely to open up. If this doesn't help, and they continue their silence, get help.

Why should I call a suicide prevention center? What can they do over the phone?

The counselors at these centers are trained to talk with people in crisis. They generally know what to say, how to say it, and when. They can also call others to come to the aid of a person in need, or if you are calling about a friend, the counselor can call the friend directly.

It needs to be made clear, however, that in some centers the philosophy is that a person has a right to choose whether they live or die. This attitude is not one that I personally support because psychologically, the person in need is desperately hoping someone will stop them from ending their life. To say to the person that it is their choice is to ignore their cry for help and not understand the psychological dynamics. Ultimately, it can become the reason for their attempt and death. We must try.

What about someone who draws pictures of a body hanging?

Remember that any reference to dying, verbal or written, can be a clue that the person is suicidal. Drawing pictures of death does not always indicate suicide, but this can't be determined until the person is asked about suicide. Drawings should be taken seriously.

I know someone who jokes about it. What do I do?

Suicide is no joke. Even people who joke about it are serious. The joking is sometimes unknowingly used because the person knows of no other way to communicate. These people often joke about everything that is serious to them.

Any reference to dying, verbal or written, can be a clue that a person is suicidal.

This girl I know never does anything she threatens to do when she's mad. How do I know if she'll do something dumb one of these times? I get tired of her.

This kind of person makes us angry after a while. We tend not to listen to or even want to spend time with them. This is a normal reaction. The anger comes from our own fear that, the one time we don't take the person seriously, they'll do something. That's a lot of pressure and makes us feel like we can't win.

The fact is that each threat must be taken seriously because the risk is high if it is ignored. It helps to sometimes say to this person, "You upset me when you keep threatening to kill yourself. I know you're mad, but why would you want to give the person you're mad at the satisfaction of saying you're crazy because of your suicide threats? It really doesn't help, and killing yourself is not likely to change much of anything. Let's go talk to someone who can help straighten things out."

This may or may not help. The threat still needs to be taken seriously. If you don't feel comfortable dealing with the person, then tell someone else who can get to them.

References

Adler, A. (1930). *The problem child*. New York: P. G. Putnam's Sons.

Alisic, E., Boeije, H. R., Jongmans, M. J., & Kleber, R. J. (2011). Children's perspectives on dealing with traumatic events. *Journal of Loss and Trauma, 16*, 477–496.

Amish School Shooting. (n.d.). In *Wikipedia*. Retrieved January 4, 2014, from http:// en.wikipedia.org/wiki/Amish_school_shooting

Boyle, L. (2013). *Extraordinary bond between grieving mother and firefighter who was last one to hold her dying baby in iconic Oklahoma City bomb photo*. Retrieved January 15, 2014, from http://www.dailymail.co.uk/news/article-2347862/Oklahoma-city-bombing-Mother-reunited-firefighter-hold-baby-daughter-iconic-Oklahoma-bombing-picture. html#ixzz2rpGwiwLF

Boyle, T. (2012). *From the depths of fear, pain, and love*. Retrieved December 12, 2013, from http://www.thehilltopecho.org/editorial/2012/03/16/from-the-depths-of-fear-pain-and-love/

Carlton, G., Markowitz, M., Haddow, J., & Steele, W. (2011). *After the crisis: Trauma event crisis intervention planning*. Clinton Twp., MI: TLC Institute (www.starr.org/training/ tlc/resources).

Carter, C. S. (2007). Neuropeptides and the protective effects of social bonds. In E. Harmon-Jones & P. Winkielman (Eds.), *Social neuroscience: Integrating biological and psychological explanations of social behavior* (pp. 425–437). New York: Guilford Press.

Centers for Disease Control and Prevention. (2011). *Adverse child experiences (ACE) study*. Retrieved March 30, 2011, from http://www.cdc.gov/ace/index.htm

Chandra, A., Lara-Cinisomo, S., Jaycox, L., Tanielian, T., Burns, R., Ruder, T., & Han, B. (2009). *Children on the homefront: The experience of children from military families*. Retrieved December 23, 2013, from http://pediatrics.aappublications.org/content/125/1/16

Clark, V., & Woodall, M. (2004, April 1). Young lives, violent deaths. *Philadelphia Inquirer*.

Davis, J. (2013). *Hypertension/high blood pressure health center*. Retrieved October 10, 2013, from http://www.webmd.com/hypertension-high-blood-pressure/features/5-ways-pets-improve-your-health

Echterling, L. G., Presbury, J. H., & McKee, J. E. (2004). *Crisis intervention: Promoting resilience and resolution in troubled times.* Upper Saddle River, NJ: Prentice Hall.

Ellen, J. (2014). *San Francisco's El Dorado Elementary uses trauma-informed & restorative practices; suspensions drop 89%.* Retrieved January 7, 2014, from http://acestoohigh.com/2014/01/28/hearts-el-dorado-elementary/

Enigma Variations. (n.d.). In *Wikipedia.* Retrieved January 23, 2014, from http://en.wikipedia.org/wiki/Enigma_Variations

Fulghum, R. (1999). *All I really need to know I learned in kindergarten.* Woodstock, IL: Dramatic Publishing Company.

Generosity. (n.d.). In *Merriam-Webster Online Dictionary.* Retrieved October 1, 2013, from http://www.merriam-webster.com/dictionary/generosity

Giovanni, N. (2007). *We remember: Transcript of Nicki Giovanni's convocation address.* Retrieved December 22, 2013, from http://www.remembrance.vt.edu/2007/archive/giovanni_transcript.html

Goodwin, J. (2013, December / 2014, January). *Sandy Hook grandparents share stories.* Retrieved January 20, 2014, from http://www.aarp.org/home-family/friends-family/info-12-2013/newtown-grandparents-grieve-loss.html

Henry, J. (2011). *Stuffed animals may ease war-related stress in kids.* Retrieved June 4, 2012, from http://www.reuters.com/article/2008/01/11/us-stuffed-kids-idUSHAR16990320080111

Huffington Post Parents. (2013). *'Look for the helpers': Quote from Mr. Rogers that we really need right now.* Retrieved February 12, 2014, from http://www.huffingtonpost.com/2013/04/15/mr-rogers-look-for-the-helpers_n_3088716.html

Jaworski, J. (1998). *Synchronicity: The inner path of leadership.* San Francisco, CA: BK Publishers.

Joseph, S. (2011). *What doesn't kill us: The new psychology of posttraumatic growth.* Philadelphia, PA: Basic Books.

Levine, P., & Kline, M. (2008). *Trauma proofing your kids.* Berkeley, CA: North Atlantic Books.

McFarlane, A., Policansky, S., & Irwin, C. (1987). A longitudinal study of the psychological morbidity in children due to a natural disaster. *Psychological Medicine, 17,* 727–738.

Montimurri, P., & Braiser, L. (2013). *Therapy dogs help calm people under stress.* Retrieved November 11, 2013, from http://www.usatoday.com/story/news/nation/2013/02/16/therapy-dogs-calm-people-under-stress/1925293/

National Association of School Psychologists. (2002). *Memorials/activities/rituals following traumatic events: Suggestions for schools.* Retrieved December 14, 2013, from http://www.nasponline.org/resources/crisis_safety/memorials_general.aspx

National Association of School Psychologists. (2011). *Memorials: Special considerations when memorializing an incident (WS1 Handout 21).* Retrieved November 2, 2013, from http://www.nasponline.org/resources/crisis_safety/w_WS1H21_Memorials.pdf

National Center for Trauma Informed Care. (2011). *What's trauma-informed care?* Retrieved June 30, 2011, from http://www.samhsa.gov/nctic/trauma.asp

Pain, C. (2007). *Paying tribute to deceased school community members.* Retrieved October 22, 2013, from http://rems.ed.gov/docs/ERCMNewsletter_Memorials.pdf

Payne, S. L. (2014). *The drum circle.* Retrieved August 10, 2014, from http://www.youtube.com/watch?v=pdN6olQXHyo

Perry, B. (2009). Examining child maltreatment through a neurodevelopmental lens: Clinical applications of the neurosequential model of therapeutics. *Journal of Loss and Trauma*, 14(4), 16.

Ratey, J. J. (2002). *A user's guide to the brain: Perception, attention, and the four theatres of the brain*. New York: Vintage Books.

Raven, K. (2013). *Military deployments tied to teens' depression*. Retrieved November 22, 2013, from http://www.reuters.com/article/2013/11/29/us-military-depression-idUSBRE9AS0P120131129

Rothschild, B. (2000). *The body remembers: The psychophysiology of trauma and trauma treatment*. New York: W. W. Norton.

Steele, W. (2005). *Interventions following suicide and other traumatic situations*. Clinton Twp., MI: TLC Institute: 57–62 (www.starrtraining.org/training/tlc/resources).

Steele, W. (2013). *Critical considerations: TLC recovery interventions following traumatic incidents*. Clinton Twp., MI: TLC Institute (www.starrtraining.org/training/tlc/resources).

Steele, W., & Hayak, M. (2013). *Adults and parents in trauma*. (Revised). Clinton Twp., MI: TLC Institute (www.starrtraining.org/training/tlc/resources).

Steele, W., & Jacobs, J. (2007). *Structured sensory interventions for at-risk and adjudicated adolescents*. Clinton Twp., MI: TLC Institute (www.starrtraining.org/training/tlc/resources).

Steele, W., & Kuban, C. (2013). *Working with grieving and traumatized children and adolescents: Discovering what matters most through evidence-based, sensory interventions*. Hoboken, NJ: John Wiley & Sons.

Steele, W., Kuban, C., Lemerand, P., & Ginns-Gruenberg, D. (2007). *I feel better now*. Clinton Twp., MI: TLC Institute (www.starrtraining.org/training/tlc/resources).

Steele, W., & Malchiodi, M. (2012). *Trauma-informed practices for children and adolescents*. New York: Routledge.

Steele, W., & Raider, M. (2001). *Structured sensory interventions for children, adolescents and parents (SITCAP)*. New York: Edwin Mellen Press.

Taylor, M. (1999). *Imaginary companions and the children who create them*. New York: Oxford University Press.

Therapy dog. (n.d.). In *Wikipedia*. Retrieved October 8, 2013, from http://en.wikipedia.org/wiki/Therapy_dog

van der Kolk, B. A., McFarlane, A. C., & Weisaeth, L. (Eds.) (1996). *Traumatic stress: The effects of overwhelming experience on mind, body, and society*. New York: Guilford Press.

Zak, P. J., Stanton, A. A., & Ahmadi, S. (2007). *Oxytocin increases generosity in humans*. PLoS ONE, 2(11), e1128. doi:10.1371/journal.pone.0001128

Index